David Lloyd

The wonderful, surprising, and uncommon Voyages and

Adventures of Captain Jones

David Lloyd

The wonderful, surprising, and uncommon Voyages and Adventures of Captain Jones

ISBN/EAN: 9783742886811

Manufactured in Europe, USA, Canada, Australia, Japa

Cover: Foto ©Andreas Hilbeck / pixelio.de

Manufactured and distributed by brebook publishing software (www.brebook.com)

David Lloyd

The wonderful, surprising, and uncommon Voyages and

Adventures of Captain Jones

THE

Wonderful, Surprizing and Uncommon

VOYAGES

AND

ADVENTURES

OF

CAPTAIN JONES

To PATAGONIA.

RELATING

His Adventure to Sea. His firſt landing, and ſtrange combat with a mighty bear. His furious battle with his ſix and thirty men, againſt an army of eleven kings, with their overthrow and deaths. His relieving of Kemper Caſtle. His ſtrange and admirable ſea fight with ſix huge galleys of Spain, and nine thouſand ſoldiers. His being taken priſoner, and hard uſage. His being ſet at liberty by the king's command, in exchange for twenty-four Spaniſh captains, and return for England. A comical deſcription of Captain JONES's ruby noſe. Part the Second. His incredible adventures and atchievements by ſea and land, particularly his miraculous deliverance from a wreck at ſea, by the ſupport of a dolphin. His ſeveral deſperate duels. His combat with BAHADAR CHAM, a giant of the race of OG. His loves with the queen of NO-LAND, and baſely leaving her. His deep employments, and happy ſucceſs in buſineſs of ſtate.

All which, and more, is but the Tythe of his own Relation, which he continued until he grew Speechleſs and Died.

With his ELEGY and EPITAPH.

The SECOND EDITION.

LONDON:

Printed for JOHN LEVER, Bookſeller, Stationer, and Printſeller, at Little Moorgate, next to London Wall, near Moorfields. MDCCLXVI.

(Price One Shilling.)

FAME's windy trump blew up this haughty
        mind,
To do, or wish to do, what here you find :
'Twas ne'er held error yet in errant Knights
(Which privilege he claims) to dress their fights
In high hyperbolies : for youth's example,
To make their minds, as they grow men, grow
        ample.
Thus such atchievements are assay'd and done,
As pass the common power and sense of man.
Then let high spirits strive to imitate,
Not what he did, but what he doth relate.

To the R E A D E R.

REader, you've here the mirror of the times,
 Old Jones wrapp'd in his colours, and my
 rhimes.
Receive him fairly, pray ; nor cenfure how,
Or what he tells ; the matter he'll avow.
And for the form he fpeaks in, I'll maintain it,
It comes as near his vein as I could ftrain it.
For 'twere improper to fet forth an afs
Caprifon'd, and pannel a great horfe.
My part claims no invention's praife : for (know it)
Where ere there's fiction in't, there he's the poet.
His laft deeds here epitomiz'd, intreat
Some thundering pen to fet them forth compleat.
Let him whofe lofty Mufe will deign to do it,
Drink fack and gunpowder, and fo fall to it.

After

After Captain ·Jones his great Conqueſt in the Indies, theſe Verſes were engraven on a Pillar of Gold, in the famous City of Chiapa.

Havacun! *at ſiquinta,* *rucar,* *ruchaquit, a holom,*
Rutſi nutſiquin Jonos, *quintacque* Britanno ;
In rutiſba Dios, *chiru narapata tiquita,*
Xalocobta naloc quinquimi, nava tinuloc,
Chaquil Ruchaquil, Don Spanos, *Cacaracarta*
Inra Ixnulocoſh Europon *quincol amolob,*
Chinaloconta nucam quiti Chicata Chiapa,
Mecoacana mani quinraphi tilcona rutat,
Inrurapa cochor vilcat Cacunta, Chalocch
Havocobta ruvac, Rixim car nucar avixim ;
Ixlocon-bita quimac, avix inreca corochi,
Pan Nutſi nuchac, quinrochi nutiſba China ;
Chipam Rumolobimac, numac taxa veronquil
Chyrvo capat quiro vinac navecata maniquir,
Chilocontho Navos nutacqui Coave-caca,
Quinvani vilquin Xinvi nucamca tivito.

By the aſſiſtance of Mr. Gage *his rules to learn that* Indian *Tongue, called* Poconchi, *thus faithfully and verbatim tranſlated into* Engliſh.

HO paſſenger! Behold, read, underſtand,
Great Jones a Briton conquer'd all this land ;
In thirteen days twelve Kings he overthrew,
And millions of ſavages he ſlew :
At laſt the Spaniſh Dons, with all their force
Of Indian foot, and European horſe,

Sur-

Surpriz'd him near Chiapa, where he ftood
Five hours in fight cover'd with fire and blood ;
And in that furious conflict all his men,
Who were once thirty-fix reduc'd to ten ;
With thofe few blades, and his own mighty arm,
He did repulfe them without fpell or charm :
Then to his fhip retreated ; and to fhew,
'Twas glory and not gold he did purfue ;
　Of all the fpoils he took but one rich cup,
　And as much gold as made this pillar up.

This monument ftood undefac'd 1588. But immediately after was demolifhed by the envy of the Spaniards, and the gold converted to other ufes.

E. LL.

On the Revival of Captain JONES.

WHY fhak'ft thou coward hand, do'ft drop
　　　the pen,
Honour'd to limn the prodigy of men ?
What means this ftrange furprifal that unknits
Thy joints, poffeffing them with palfy'd fits ?
Who dares (dread hero) offer to thy fame,
(Without Apollo's call) muft feel the fame.
Mov'd by pure zeal to honour, thus I run,
A young enthufiaft the priefts among,
Trembling to pay my mite. Welcome once more
To us, Great Britain's Mars ; our joys run o'er,
To fee the truth of a platonic year
Confirm'd in thee ; fo bright do'ft thou appear,
Deck'd with thy valour's rays : poets (who can
Make gods) have rais'd thee up thou god-like man.
What brave revenge had'ft th' ad on thy old foe,
Had'ft thou but breath'd our air fome months ago ?
Thou, and thy fix-and-thirty fet on fhore
In Hifpaniola, would'ft have acted more

Than

Than was (I blufhing write it) done by ——
And——with their ten thoufand men.
I acquiefce, and leave to higher forms,
Thy ftern deportment in all fights and ftorms,
Who draw at large, and well ; my fingle hint
Is a portentous act in a fmall print.
Reward thofe who again have made thee breathe,
With laurel ta'en from thy victorious wreathe ;
I have enough t'entitle me to fame,
Who both a Briton am, and of thy name.

H. I.

---

*A Supplement to the famous Hiſtory of the truly
valiant and magnanimous Captain* JONES.

LOOK to yourfelves. I fee his marble frown,
His threat'ning afhes challenge their renown,
Expoftulating thus. Durft your narration,
Omit thofe noble acts of admiration,
Which I perform'd, when Æolus deny'd
Me his affiftance 'gainft the ftruggling tide ?
Never was martial man affronted worfe,
Tyrone had brib'd him to retort my courfe.
Some wifh'd me fent to Lapland for a wind,
Nay that I fcorn'd, I had enough behind ;
Turning my poftern, I fent forth a blaft
That tore the fails, and crack'd the fturdy maft,
Hurrying my frigate with fuch force, that it
Ran on a fhelve, and fo was like to fplit.
'Gramercy policy, this I forefaw,
For fuch mifchances I had help at maw ;
I'd drank an ocean up of Englifh beer,
Which (wanting water) I made ufe of here ;
I turn'd my conduit pipe o'er deck and fpouted,
And fill'd the fhore, fo that Saint Patrick fhouted,

And

And cry'd, my friends this is no time for mirth,
Oh honey! a deluge comes to drown the earth!
Obstructions being removed in this sort,
At length I landed in an Irish port,
And thought it wisdom, before they came to treat,
To stay my stomach with a bit of meat.
Seeing a cook hang up a stall-fed ox,
I bid him roast him quickly, with a pox;
'Twas quickly done: as soon as off the spit,
My valiant grinders snapt it at a bit;
Sooner than one could turn his hand about,
As when a pickrel swallows up a trout.
The cook's amaz'd: what quoth I, thou thief,
I do not eat, but barrel up my beef;
I can lay up a whole one and a half,
The Ox that Milo carried was a calf:
Sirrah make haste, get me some more meat dress'd,
To fortify the castle of my breast.
I mean to feed as dromedaries do,
Both for the present and the future too.
Thus terrify'd, my foes ran to the bogs,
And there were metamorphos'd into frogs;
I speedily destroy'd that croaking faction,
Then could no longer live for want of action.
Death, nature's beadle, took me by the hand,
And said, Grand Captain I thee now disband,
Abstract of valour, let thy name be blest,
Lye down within this tomb, and take thy rest.

R. LL.

On Valiant J O N E S.

COME see the man, whom mountains bred,
Who talked high, as he was fed.
No court-like milk-sop train'd to th' fiddle,
But ye and i' th' region call'd the middle.

There

There Captain Jones his cradle choofes,
More dangerous than that of Mofes ;
For that was watch'd by Pharaoh's daughter,
The De'el a nurfe did him look after,
Or he for them : come wolf or goat
Who took the Nib, and fill'd his throat,
Thence was ally'd to Brute ; near cuz
By th' nurfe's fide to Romulus :
And for his nimblenefs and fkipping,
Remus (himfelf) could ne'er out leap him;
This, and the warbles of his throat,
Came from the rennet of the goat
Curdling his gutturals : his hair's
All flaggy too, and rank as theirs.
Which was refented, as was Mars
Or Hercules for his black A——
Thefe were ftrange figns, and did betoken,
What e'er was after by him fpoken.
'Twas well the wars were done before,
Loft in Llwellin and Glendore.
Had Jones liv'd then, in vain th' affails
Of Saxons ; Wales had ftill been Wales.

　　Nay, had the Fates (but they deny'd,
For Jones had neither bairn nor bride)
Sav'd but his præpuce in Skink's fight,
That fpoil'd his fkirmifhes by night,
No doubt an iffue, not of's legs,
But of his loins, for he lov'd eggs,
Extremely to the very bowels,
Would have out Vavaford the Powels:
Content us therefore with thofe duels,
Which no man did, or very few elfe,
Related from his mouth : this Brit,
A's Cæfar did, could he have writ,
What comments had he made ? what ftories
Of Irifh wolves which now are Tories :
This Frontifpiece alas ! nay twenty, .
As big as this had been too fcanty,

The

The elephant and's Pego-man,
And Hobb on his Leviathan,
Nay, what so ere old Inigo
(His name-sake) could have drawn for show,
Had been too small a scene; why then,
No more, it shrivels up my pen.

ON THE

Wonderful Voyages of Captain JONES.

READER, be stout and credulous, for he
   Must have both courage and credulity,
That reads this Poem; and to have enough,
His soul should be half Cheverell and half Buff:
For Jones such things doth talk, and such things do,
As far transcend all faith and reason too.
   That antient Poets, that in former times,
Extoll'd their Heroes with undying Rhimes;
Must go to school to learn of Jones, for he,
At once both made and writ all Chivalry.
There Homer and Achilles both must club
To make one story, this must fight, that dub.
Which asks Time, Charge and Danger; whilst bold Jones,
Does without either raise, and kill at once;
Tam Marti quam Mercurio, if he list,
He could dispute, as well as fight with fist.
With on Cuff-syllogism confute more men,
Than Wit or Reason could convince with ten.
   'Mong all the Giants whom he robb'd of breath,
He has three signal Battles fought with Death,
While Fame, that still hates living men, gave out,
That Jones was conquer'd; and to clear the doubt,
Employ'd

Employ'd the Wits with a lamenting pen,
In Epitaphs to kill him o'er again.
    At which enrag'd he rofe, and fwore they lye;
    Jones is not dead; I fwear Jones fhall not dye.

A B.

Upon Captain JONES *relating his own Exploits.*

LO here great Captain Jones! in whom do dwell,
    Both Mars and Mercury, Gods ftout and fell;
Thou, thine own Trump, doft with a valiant voice,
Both beat thy foes, and thy great conquefts noife;
Thus thy Minerva lends thee fpeech and fhield,
Wherewith thou all things mak'ft unto thee yield;
Ajax, Ulyffes, both in thee agree,
Thy valour and thy tongue alike are free;
Great Alexander's envy would have ceaft,
Nor would Achilles' fate have fpoil'd his reft,
Had but Jones's Poetry infpir'd his foul,
To whom the blind man Homer's but a fool;
Homer cou'd only his borrow'd fancy write,
Jones cou'd do more, both ftrangely fain and fight
Cæfar of all the Worthy's moft like thee,
He did both fight and tell's own Hiftory.
Which yet compar'd with thy relation,
Seems but an old thread-bare narration;
So between both, how vaft's the difference,
Jones doth all Cæfar's baffle, and all fenfe.

B b 2   I. V. Oxon.

On.

On the Same.

AWAY with Fictions, short of our stout man,
 The Poet must now turn Historian;
His fights, his fights, his fights, his victories,
His conquests, his trophies, and yet no lies!
What wars were they when all each battle fell,
But Jones, and he surviv'd, his services to tell!
When he relates the story, an enemy
Truth fears to be, left in contending she,
Too late learn due subjection; thus the tide
Forces the waters that would gently slide:
When our great Jones, had quite subdu'd the land,
He boldly puts to sea; but here's a stand;
The sea of such an adversary proud
To try'm, its waves into a storm doth crowd.
Jones leaves his ship, he scorned such a flood,
For he had often swam in streams of blood;
He then such tempests rais'd with arms and back,
That th' very ocean did fear a wreck.
Yet he would die, that th' shades might of him fear,
And learn, by mortals woe, great Jones to fear.

       N. H.

Upon the incomparable valiant, Captain JONES.

WHEN I do read thy Travels, Jones, and see
 Thy Fights, thy Victories, thy All, and Thee,
I stand engag'd 'twixt wonder and delight,
That I can neither think, nor speak, nor write.
My faith thou puzzl'st, and invention too,
'Tis monstrous strange! but these things thou did'st
 do;

       Alcides,

Alcides, Hector, are out-done by thee,
Thy Hiftory hath foil'd all Poetry.
Poor Hector! he by his own valour's loft,
But thou furviv'ft, and doft thy triumphs boaft.
Herc'les, we know, hath his Non ultra found,
But to thee, Jones, nor earth, nor fea's a bound;
The world from eaft to weft, from north to fouth,
To eccho forth thy fame's but one wide mouth.
The earth, great Jones, grows fruitful in thy praife,
And all her care's to crown thy head with bays.
The fea pays homage to thee, and roars out,
Brave Jones's name, who's greater far than Cnute.
Neptune to thee his trident doth refign,
The whales cry out with trembling, We are thine;
And proud of thy command, they fwell the main,
For thy great fake thronging into a train;
Then Spain does yield to thy fierce heat; thy might
Proftrates their doughty Don, Diego height;
Thy arms fo tofs'd that vap'ring Admiral,
As if had nought been but a Tennis-ball.
Thou did'ft Bears, Lions, and fuch Monfters quell;
By thy ftrong hand the fturdy El'phant fell.
Ere the bright fun peep'd from his eaftern bed,
Eleven Kings before thy feet, brave Jones, lay dead.
What work would'ft thou have made in one whole
　　day,
Had'ft thou but found for thy Killzadog play?
How fuch exploits, fo ftrange, thou could'ft atchieve,
None ever yet could tell brave Jones, and live.
Poor mortals we! the Fates have thought it fit,
We fhould in wonder fpend our days and wit.

P. D. Ox.

HAVE

HAVE you not heard of Jones, that man of
      wonder,
That brought Don Dego and Mac-kill Cow under?
And when he had 'um there agreed, being wife,
To run away before that they fhould rife?
For 'tis a maxim; If youl'd be fecure,
Still make the reliques of a conqueft fure:
Jones ftill kill'd thofe that fled, and only thofe;
For fuch tuff fellows as withftood his blows
He fcorn'd and fpar'd; thinking it bafe to beat,
A ftubborn enemy that won't retreat.
  'Mongft all thofe bluftering Sirs that I have read
(Whofe greateft wonder is that they are dead)
There's not any Knights, nor bold Atchiver's Name,
So much as Jones's in the Book of Fame:
They much of Greece's Alexander brag,
He'd put ten Alexanders in a bag:
Eleven fierce Kings, backt with two thoufand Louts,
Jones with a ragged troop beats all to clouts.
But fure it was a conqueft by compact,
For he could never be accus'd of fact:
And yet no ftory a Romancer fings,
That ere exploited more ftupendous things;
Quixote a winged Giant once did kill,
That's but a flying tale, believ't who will:
This were but pretty hardfhip, Jones was one,
Would fkin a flint, and eat him when h' had done.
  Had Jones but been alive and feen the pudder,
Betwixt Briganza's Legate and Anftrudder;
When the fierce Portugal in high bravado,
(Storming th' Exchange with piftols and granado)
Put the poor Pego-mongers to a rout,
And their beloved Baubles flung about:
He'd not have fawn'd upon him like a fpaniel,
Jones would have kickt the dog into the kennel;
And fpight of darknefs made his head ring noon,
For daring to pluck honour from the moon:
                         H' had

H' had died no other death, for furious Jones,
Once flesh'd, would kill ten such and make no
    bones.
He once had an encounter with a lion,
(Though most believe he never durst come nigh one)
But as the Author says, and I believe,
Both bravely fought, and many wounds did give
Each other, 'till the beast in woeful dumps
Worne out, (for Jones had fought him to his stumps)
In honour of his fall and Jones's glory,
Died with meer age, and there's an end of th' story.
Many a tough adventure he hath had,
And like a true Knight Errant, ne'er a bad :
He foil'd great Asdriasdust in the twink-
Ling of an eye, as easy as to drink :
And yet as tough, and dry a fir, as ere was yok't
Unto a sword (Jones often wisht him chok't)
But yet of all the Giants that came nigh him,
There's Nerapenny stuck the longer by him ;
For though his slender wounds made many doubt
    him,
That threadbare Tearcoats he had still about him ;
And if they say he had not, he's bely'd,
For he had ne'er a penny when he dy'd.
Jones had a valiant stomach, and would eat,
As well as fight, provided he had meat,
Else patience upon force took place, for Jones
Kept many fasting days, and made no bones.
But I'd not have you think it was for want ;
For when he had no money, nor provant,
The fowl flew to his table, and the fish
Left the cold stream, and swam into his dish.
'Tis an old Proverb, (like to like they say)
Jones was a Cod's-head too as well as they.
But Jones, like a disease, both sexes smites ;
For he wounds Ladies too as well as Knights :
                          He

He was fo trim a youth, the Queen of No-land,
Thought him fome Princely Shaver come from
    Poland ;
And fo he prov'd indeed, for by Guds duds,
He moft unkindly left her in the Suds ;
Jones like a Wifeacre begg'd to be fpar'd,
For he had No-land, nor for No-land car'd :
If any ask you wherein lay his Grace ?
Venus lov'd Mars his Truncheon not his face.

   To wind up all, Fame's Trump his Deeds doth
    tell,
   Although a fow-gelder's would do't as well.

                        W. T.

THE

The Wonderful and Surprizing

VOYAGES

OF

CAPTAIN JONES

To PATAGONIA.

Sing thy arms (Bellona) and the Man's,
I Whofe mighty deeds out-did great Tam-
berlan's :
Thy trump, dire goddefs, fend, that I
may thunder,
Some wond'rous ftrain, to fpeak this man of wonder.
  When fates decreed that Captain Jones fhould be
The life and death of men, they could not fee
A place more fuiting to bring forth this mirror,
Of martial fpirits, this thunder-crack of terror,
Than fome vaft mountain's womb, whofe rigid
rocks
Might form him, and forefhew the hardy knocks
Which he fhould give and take : nor were they nice
To think it bafe, that mountains bring forth mice ;
Since from a Britifh mount, and Mars's ftones,
They fent this man of men, 'ftern Captain Jones.
Wild maresmilk nurs'd him on the mountain's gorfe,
Which gave him ftrength and ftomach like a horfe ;

C   Goats

Goats flesh matur'd him, kill'd on craggy tops,
Which taught him to mount rampiers like those
   rocks.
Ere eighteen winters fully waxen were,
This imp of Mars began to do and dare.
With Reymond, a stout brother of the sword,
He first attempted sea, and went abroad ;
Two hundred strong, for the East Indies bound,
Fame was the only prize he sought or found.
Twice twenty days auspicious waves and winds
Lull'd them : then Æolus and Neptune joins
To work great Jones's fall.   Envy and ire,
To see him more than man, made them conspire :
Rough Boreas whistled to the dancing ship,
The boisterous billows strove to over skip
The bounding vessel.   In this great disaster,
Reymond, the soldiers, mariners and master,
Lost heart and heed to rule ; then up starts Jones,
Calls for six gills, drinks them off at once.
Thus arm'd at all points, yet as light as feather,
He ascends, and drew, and piss'd against the weather;
And are we born (my hearts, quoth he) to die ?
Shall we descend ? Thy immortality,
Neptune, thou must resign, if I come thither :
One sea may not contain us both together.
Nor waves, nor winds, could fright him with the
   motion,
Who thought he could contain and piss an ocean.
His fatal Smiter thrice aloft he shakes,
And frowns ; the sea and ship and canvas quakes :
Then from the hatches he descends, and stept
Into his cabin, drank again, and slept.
When these rough gods beheld him thus secure,
And arm'd against them, like a man pot-sure ;
They stint vain storms; and so Monstrifera *
(So hight the ship) touch'd about Florida ;

Upon

---

* The name of his ship.

Upon a defart ifland call'd Crotona,
Where favage beafts and ferpents live alone :
Here Joneswhoneedswouldland,tho'Reymondfwore
Danger was in't ; he laugh'd and leap'd afhore.
Danger (quoth he) to them whom danger fright,
My heart was fram'd to dare, my hands to fight.
Some fix and thirty more put forth to ground,
Thefe for frefh food, he for adventure bound ;
They limit their return when three hours ends,
Which Reymond, with the fhip, at fea attends.
Thefe fea-fick foldiers, rang hills, woods, and vallies,
Seeking provant to fill their empty bellies ;
Jones goes alone, where fate prepar'd to meet him,
With fuch a prey as did unfriendly greet him ;
A bear as black as darknefs, and as fell
As tyger, vaft as the black dog of hell,
Runs at him open jaw'd, fo fierce, fo faft,
That he no leifure had to draw for hafte.
* Kilzadog, his good fword, with fift he aim'd,
Alarm'd, a blow which fure the bear had brain'd ;
But that between her yawning teeth it dings,
The gauntlet there ftuck faft, his hands he wrings,
Unarm'd, unarm'd from thence; her foremoft paws,
The bear on Jones's fhoulder claps, and gnaws
The gauntlet wedg'd between her teeth : Jones
       clafp'd her
With both his arms, and ftrove by force to caft her.
And here they try a pluck, and grafp, and tug,
And foam ; but Jones who knew the Cornifh hug,
Heaves her a foot from footing, fwings her round,
And with a fhort turn hurls her on the ground ;
Then came his good fword forth to act his part,
Which pierc'd fkin, ribs, and riffe, and rove her
       heart.
The head (his trophy) from the trunk he cuts,
And with it back unto the fhore he ftruts,

C 2   Where

* The name of his fword.

Where Reymond was appointed to attend
His and the rests return: but he (false friend)
When they were once on shore and out of sight,
Hoist sails to sea, and took himself to flight.
Here Jones found fraud in man, and deeply swears
Revenge on Reymond's head, the rest he cheers;
All safe return'd, but all in desperation,
To see themselves left there to desolation:
Nor grain, nor ground, but wild; nor man, nor beast,
But savage; yet (O strange) here Jones doth feast
His six and thirty daily, 'twas with fishes,
Tost from his halbert's point into their dishes;
Wherewith he took them standing on the shore
Out of the ocean; whether 'twas the store,
Frequenting this unpeopled coast, or whether,
To see this wond'rous man they shoal'd together;
And so astonish'd, yield themselves a prey,
To him from whom they durst not swim away.
Be't so, or so, I'll not decide, but I
Know Jones tells this for truth, who knows no lye.
Thus from his weapon's point, nine months they fed,
Till fate Sir Richard Greenfield thither led;
Who to America transports, with Jones,
His six and thirty fish-fed Mermidons.
To Insip were they brought and left; oh then
'Twas time, had they had meat, to play the men.
Their first encounter there with famine was,
A dry and desart soil, nor grain, nor grass,
Nor drink, but water had they here, nor bread,
For thrice twelve months, but caves for house and
        bed.
Such living as that country could afford,
Bold Jones was forc'd to win by dint of sword.
* Eleven fierce Kings possess the fertile tract
Of this great coast, who all their powers compact
To vanquish Jones: a brave attempt, 'tis true,
Yet more than twice eleven fierce Kings could do.

Two

* Captain Jones encounters with the giants Astiriasdust.

Two thoufand choice and doughty men they chofe,
To bid him battle, arm'd with darts and bows,
And arrows fathom long, well barb'd with bone,
Of fome ftrange fifh, which pierc'd through fteel
    and ftone ;
And thus they came prepar'd. When they drew
    near him,
He brought his foldiers forth, and thus did cheer
    them ;
My five and twenty friends (for only thofe
Had fate and famine left) thefe darts and bows,
Are fit to deal with fearful Crows and Daws ;
But us, whofe hearts of oak and empty maws,
Hunger's fharp dart hath pierc'd (and yet we ftand
To fright and foil our foes with fword in hand)
Thefe weapons cannot conquer, nor the number
Were they two thoufand fuch as John-a-Cumber.
Doth hunger bite you ? bite your foes as faft,
Eat thefe men-eaters (foldiers) kill and tafte.
Would you gain glory ? kill by fix and feven,
If crowns of Kings, then here behold eleven.
And this he fpake and drew. With ftomach fierce
They give the firft affault. Now for a verfe,
To fpeak great Jones's deeds, who headlong goes
Amongft the thickeft ranks, cuts, kills, and throws,
Some by the legs, fome by the wafte he makes
Shorter ; another by the lock he takes,
Reaps off his head, wherewith he brains another,
Then at one ftroke, kills father, fon, and brother ;
Few 'fcap'd with life, but ftrangely ; happy thofe,
Which 'fcap'd with lofs of half a face or nofe.
Nor may I pafs his men, who cut and flafh,
Like thofe that fought for life, not crowns or cafh.
Want made them feem (which fure their foes dif-
    maid)
The very fons of death whofe parts they play'd ;
The Infips now no aim can take aright,
They think each foe they meet, a mighty fpright ;
                And

And so they fly. Six Kings he took, and kill'd,
Five, with eight hundred foldiers left the field ;
Twelve hundred fell : for thofe that went off fafe,
Their heels and not their hearts the praife he gave.
Unto their fulleft towns, when he had kill'd them,
He brought his ragged regiment, and fill'd them.
Here on the river of Mengog they find,
A wear with fifh of wond'rous growth and kind,
Where with a thoufand herrings they were fed,
All two foot long befides the tail and head.

Here fome may afk, what came of all the wealth,
(For Jones brought nothing home befides himfelf)
This conqueft gain'd, fure many precious things,
Muft needs attend the death of fix fuch Kings ?
I anfwer briefly ; his heroick defire
Afcends above earth excrements as fire :
Nor can defcend to crowns. The foldiers found
Much wealth, which in their home-return was
     drown'd.

Still fortune favours Jones. Amidft this river,
He fpies a fail directly bearing thither ;
He calls, and finds them Englifh, homeward bound,
Who for frefh water thruft into the Sound.
With thefe his men and he for England comes,
Had England known it, all her guns and drums
Had been too little to exprefs her joy,
As when victorious Hector enter'd Troy ;
Yet ere he can attain his native coaft,
Ænæas-like he muft be tir'd and toft
With ftorms, till meat and water wax'd fo fcant,
That Jones drank nought but pifs one week for want.
At laft when they had caft out all their goods,
(To fave themfelves) into the furious floods ;
The fhip all bruis'd with fands, and ftorms, and
     ftones,
At Ipfwich doth difburthen the fea of Jones.
England falutes him with the general joys,
Of court and country, knights, 'fquires, fools and
     boys.   In

In every town rejoice at his arrival,
The townsmen where he comes their wives do swive
    all;
And bid them think on Jones amidst this glee,
In hope to get such roaring boys as he:
Others this joy, into a fury rapp'd,
To sing his praise, though elegant and apt;
Yet mix'd with fictions, which he scorns. 'Tis
    known
Jones fancies no additions but his own;
Nor need we stir our brains for glorious stuff
To paint his praise, himself hath done enough;
And hath prescrib'd that I should write no more,
Than his good memory hath kept in store,
Of what he did.   Perhaps he hath or can
Do more, but hides it like a modest man.
His British expedition makes me hie
From his vagary to his chivalry.
This Dukedom's confines pointing on the south,
Great Keeper Castle guards on Morlig's mouth;
Which key of Britain's (like Great Britain's Dover)
Was well-nigh lost by siege till Jones went over,
To dye or raise it; 'twas begirt by land
With fifteen thousand.   Four tall ships withstand
All succours from the sea: against this force,
He goes as boldly as an eyeless horse,
With one small bark (the Shit-fire 'twas) a hot one,
And save a hundred men was with him not one:
But these were Welch blades, born for hacks and
    hewing,
And car'd not what they did so they were doing.
Thus like some tempests these four ships he frigh-
    tens,
His guns roar thunder whilst his powder lightens;
And from his broad-side pours a shower of hail,
Which rakes them through and through, ribs,
    masts, and sail.
                  Their

Their fhot replies, but they were rank'd too high,
To touch the Pinnace, which bears up fo nigh ;
And plays fo hot, that her opponents think,
Some devil is grand captain of the Pink.
One Englifh pirate with them, whilft he watches
His time to fhoot, 'fpies Jones upon the hatches ;
And cries out, Ho, hoift canvafs all at once,
And fly, or yield ; Zounds'it is Captain Jones :
The man fwore reafon, and 'twas quickly heard,
For, not a bullet, like that name was fear'd ;
They fly, he follows, but a partial wind,
And wings of fear fav'd them, left him behind.
To Kemper he returns him, and fupplies it
With fifty men, and victuals to fuffice it
Six months : the foes by land lofe hope and heart
To oppofe this new fupply, and fo depart :
Then on the gate this title was ingraved,
Jones refcued Kemper, and the Dukedom faved.
Thus plum'd with laurel, Jones for England came,
Where George of Cumberland rapp'd with his fame ;
Woos him to be vice-general of his fleet,
Which Jones vouchfaf'd, becaufe he was to meet
Men like himfelf, the doughty Dons of Spain,
Whofe honour (or lofe all) he vow'd to gain.
And better fate in this defign he wifhed not,
Than to cope fingle with their great Don Quixote.
Stay Mufe and blufh, and figh and fing no more,
Here Jones's miftrefs, Fortune, play'd the whore.
Yet, whilft thou loath'd her lightnefs to rehearfe,
Let indignation make thee chide in verfe ;
Ah deity ! and blindly to go on fo,
From thy dear minion Jones, to John D'Alonfo,
Whofe out and infide is no better mettle
Than an old drum, or a bafe tinker's kettle.
And tak'ft thou him for Jones ? that glorious boy,
Whom Venus' felf would kifs (were Mars away.)
Well fickle goddefs, if thou be divine,
I'll fwear, heaven hath like earth, light feminine.

'Twas

'Twas thus, this fleet cut through the weſtern main,
And ſo lay hovering on the coaſt of Spain:
Jones led the front (as 'twas his cuſtom ſtill)
The firſt in fight, laſt to be kill'd or kill:
His ſhip went ſwiſteſt too, as did his mind
On honour's wings: but, oh! an envious wind
Fill'd all his ſail, and wrap'd him in a miſt
From being ſeen, or ſeeing, ere he wiſt.
And thus he loſt his train, and caſt about,
And beat theſe ſeas five days to find them out;
'Till in his queſt it was his fate to meet,
Don John D'Alonſo with the Spaniſh fleet.
This general bid amain, and Jones defy'd
From cannon's mouth.   The Don again reply'd
" With four for one. Ah Jones, had I my wiſh,
" Some godhead ſhould have turn'd thee to a fiſh,
" To eſcape this dire aſſault; thou ſhould'ſt not then,
" Be taken like a tame beaſt in thy den."
Nine thouſand ſoldiers was the force that fought
This day with Jones, whom ſix huge gallies brought,
The ſtouteſt boats to make a bold bravado,
That were in Spain's Invincible Armado:
Jones firſt commands his men to take their victual,
He ſoldier-like drank much, and pray'd a little;
Then tells them briefly, here's no place to fly,
Come friends, let's bravely live or bravely die.
By this the gallies had incloſ'd him round,
And ſought to board him; but they quickly found,
The ſhip too hot to grapple with ſo ſoon,
And ſo bore off again, and paid her room.
Then each by turn preſent her the broad-ſide,
Which ſhe repaid with inc'reſt, and ſo ply'd,
That where her bullets pierce, whole ſtreams of blood
Spout through the gallies ribs, and dye the flood;
The foes diſdain thus long to ſtand in fight
'Gainſt one, and ſo preſs on with all their might:
And now the ſtorm grew hot, and deep in blood,
" Mad rage had got the place where reaſon ſtood:"

D

Guns,

Guns, drums, and trumpets ftop the foldiers ears,
From hearing cries and groans ; and fury rears
This fatal combat to fo ftrange a height,
That higher powers exprefs th' effects of fright.
Great Neptune quak'd and roar'd, clouds ran and pift,
The winds fell down, and Titan lurk'd in mift.
Then belch huge bullets forth, fmoak, fire, and
   thunder ;
Their fury ftrikes the gods with fear and wonder.
One galley which two hundred flaves did row,
Affront the fhip in hope to bulge her prow.
Jones gave her leave ; but when fhe once came nigh,
One burft his murd'ring fhot ; here doom'd to die,
Down dropp'd the brave viceroy of Saint Iago,
Don Diego de Cordona and Gonzago.
Stones, chains, and bullets tare their paffage out
Through men and galley, which foon tack'd about
In hope to get aloof ; but Jones fent after
Two lucky fhots, which light 'twix wind and water.
" In crept the quaking billow, where he fpy'd
" Thofe holes, in hope its fearful head to hide ;
" The galley like afraid, worfe hurt, doth creep
" Into the trembling bowels of the deep ;
" And fo fhe funk." Thus Diego, whilft he try'd
His force with Jones, with fifteen hundred dy'd.
Now Jones all breathlefs fat to take his breath
Upon a butt of fack, and drank the death
Of Don John de Alonfo, which his men,
Pledge in a rowfe, and fo they fight agen.
Ninefcore there were, but threefcore now remain
To do or fuffer, for the reft were flain.
The Spanifh force diftract 'twixt hope and fear,
Yet by their fellows fall forewarn'd, forbear
This hot affault, keep diftance, and at Jones
Let fly their fhot at random all at once,
Some half a cable fhort, and fome flew o'er
The top-fail, fome the ftern and rudder tore :
         One,

One, all the reft in fatal fury paft,
And all to fhivers rove the mafter maft,
Down fell the tackle, and the veffel lay,
An Englifh prifon and a Spanifh prey.
Starboard and larboard-fide, from poop to prow,
They all let drive, and rak'd her through and through.
All now but Jones and one man more were kill'd,
Who cry'd, Now fight and die, or live and yield.
Jones kill'd the firft, the latter he befought him,
Upon his knees, whilft by the knees he caught him
Begging for life, a bullet took away
His head, which when 'twas off ftill feem'd to pray;
Out flew the head and bullet both at once,
Between the manly thighs of captain Jones:
Who look'd behind him, art thou gone (quoth he)
Still may they die fo, that cry yield to me.
Now nought to him but blood and death appear'd,
Death was his wifh, captivity he fear'd;
Which to prevent * Kil-za-dog forth he drew,
And thus he fpake, Brave Cato, Cato flew.
And when victorious Brutus could not ftand,
He fell, but by his own victorious hand.
Brutus, I am a Brute, and have thy fpirit,
Thy fortune and felf-death I will inherit.
Thus faid, his fword unto his fide he plies,
Which his good genius ftays and thus replies:

 Hold, Jones, referv'd for thy country's good,
Born to fhed hoftile, not thy home-bred blood,
And know that felf-death is the coward's curfe,
For, he that dies fo, dies for fear of worfe;
The time will come when Irifh bogs fhall quake
Under thy feet, whilft great O'Neale doth fhake.
I may not on thy future deeds dilate,
Thy fword muft right what is involv'd in fate;
This know, in thy old age thou fhalt impart,
Unto thy country's youth thy martial art;

D 2   Teach

---

* This fword he won from the great and fearful giant Ne-
reapeny.

Teach them to manage arms, and how they muſt
Make bright their ſwords, which peace hath
   wrapp'd in ruſt.
  Now Jones vouchſaf'd to live, not for himſelf,
But for his country's good and common wealth ;
His ſcarlet cap he dons, with crimſon plume,
And he aſcends the hatches all in fume.
The muſqueteers ambitiouſly deſire
To hit this mark, and all at once give fire :
Some bullets raze his plume, his hair, his noſe,
His velvet jerkin, and his ſattin hoſe,
(The ſcars may yet be ſeen) yet draws he breath,
Fearleſs and harmleſs in the jaws of death.
  The Spaniard now conjectur'd his intent,
By ſeeking death t'avoid impriſonment,
And ſo forbore to ſhoot, drew near and ſought
To take the prey, which they ſo dear had bought.
  Then Jones all raging throws into the main,
That ſword which men and wolves and bears had
   ſlain,
That ſword which erſt had drank the blood of kings,
Into the bowels of the deep he flings.
The ocean thrill'd for fear, and gave it place,
And greedy Neptune ſnatch'd it for his mace.
Then from the ſhip he leaps amongſt his foes,
And ſo undaunted to Don John he goes,
Who bid him live, Don-like, but gave him breath,
Only to breathe in greater pains than death
This ſhock had ſent to Styx ſix thouſand men,
Whoſe ſouls Don John to ſatisfy again,
Inflicts more ſervile puniſhments on Jones,
Than countervails ſix thouſand deaths at once.
He beds on boards, is fed with bits and knocks,
Ape-like, barefoot, with neither ſhoes nor ſocks.
Hair ſhirt, blue bonnet, made a ſervile knave,
A louſy, duſty, naſty galley ſlave.
At laſt he brings Jones to the Spaniſh king,
And ſays : Great monarch, ſee this precious thing ;
                    Six

Six thousand of your braveft men he coft,
Who to gain him alive, their lives have loft,
Nor think the bargain dear, for here's a man,
Can do and fay more than your viceroys can.
This praife was given him by the crafty Don,
For fear his lofs feem'd more than what he won ;
And fo it did indeed, for Philip thought,
Jones' infide by his outfide dearly bought.
To try he afks him, whither bound, and whence
He was ; and Jones replies, with little fenfe,
Whether through fear or faining, he affords,
To all the king demands, not three wife words.
To try him further, in a goal they caft him,
Which ferv'd for nothing but to ftink and faft in.
And here it was his deftiny to light
Upon a learned prieft, a jefuit :
With him falls Jones to work.   The facred word
His weapon was, for he had drown'd his fword.
Their queftion was of purgatory, where,
And whether 'tis at all, if fo, 'tis here
(Quoth Jones.)   For he half tir'd with pains would
       needs
Go ftraight to heaven : And thus the queftion breeds.
Jones was no fchoolman, yet he bore a brain,
Which ne'er forgot what ere it could contain.
Yet this old prieft fo wrefts the letters fenfe,
Equivocates, denies plain confequence,
Starts to and fro, and raifeth fuch confufions,
That Jones' chief ward was to deny conclufions :
But, do this fubtil fchoolman what he can,
Such was the vigour of this martial man,
Though he was no good difputant or text-man,
Nor knew to fpell Amen, to ferve a fexton ;
Yet truth, with confidence and his ftrong fift,
Doth firft convince, and then convert the prieft.
Some talk of Garnets ftraw and Lipfius laffes,
Whofe miracles made many artifts affes ;

                                              But

But here's a miracle tranfcends them all,
An artift made wife by a natural.

 Now England's court rings all of Jones his fetters,
And men of rank were foon fent o'er with letters,
To ranfom him for gold, or man for man,
On any terms. The King with many a Don
Confults upon this point: one thought it fit
To deal upon exchange; fome better wit,
Thought it more fit to keep this fecond Drake,
For fo he term'd him wifely, and thus fpake;
Armies are England's arm, Captains the hand,
Of this ftrong arm that rules by fea and land :
And of this arm and hand I think in fum,
This captive Captain is the very thumb.
This fpeech was fhort and found, but could not go fo,
Without th' oppofing of old Don Mendozo;
Who lov'd and favour'd Jones, but knew not why,
(Nature it feems had wrought fome fympathy.)
 Pardon (quoth he) dread Sovereign, are we come,
To talk of arms and hands and Captain Thumb ?
From Eaft to Weft our arms and armies reign,
And fear we now for one to re-obtain,
So many viceroys in the ifle captiv'd,
For us, of light and almoft life depriv'd ;
Were Drake's and Candifh fpirit in this dragon,
Let not their future times have this to brag on,
That England's Queen did prize one Captain more,
Than Spain's great Monarch did his twenty-four.
 His fpeech prevail'd, and fo they all atone,
And twenty-four were afk'd and given for one ;
All which had led great armies to the field,
And never knew but once, what 'twas to yield.
And thus was Jones difmifs'd ; yet ere he go,
The King to grace him, made him kifs his toe.
Long may'ft thou live old man, and may thy tongue
And memory, as thou grow'ft old, wax young :
Then wilt thou live in fpite of time, and be
Time's fubject, and time thine t' emblazon thee.
        Pardon

Pardon my forward Mufe, ftriving to foar,
A pitch with thee at mid-day tir'd, gives o'er;
For, who can fpeak thee all (thou mighty man!)
Not Greece's Homer, nor Rome's Mantuan.
Thy Irifh wars, thy taking great Tyrone,
Whole herds of wolves kill'd there by thee alone,
Thy feveral fingle duels with fierce men,
And bears, all flain; and that dry journey, when
Thou drank'ft but what thou pifs'd for thrice feven
  days,
Which made thee dry ere fince, then th' amorous
  ways,
The Queen of No-land us'd to make thee King
Of her and hers (Oh!) many a precious thing.
Thy London widow next in love half drown'd,
Which thou refus'd'ft with forty thoufand pound:
Thy daunting Effex in his rafh bravado,
Raleigh's hard 'fcaping of thy baftinado:
Laftly, thy grace with thy great Queen Eliza,
Who, had'ft thou had the learning to fuffice a
Man, but to write and read, had made thee able,
To fit in council at her Highnefs' ftable.
Thefe trophies of thy fame, and myriads more,
Kept by thy fertile brain for time in ftore,
I leave unfung, and wifh they may be writ,
In golden lines by fome more happy wit,
Whofe genius, 'till fome fury doth infpire,
Let me fit down in filence, and admire.

A copious

L E T him that undertook to praife
   The French pox, and fo many ways
Did prove that it is now-a-days
                Commodious :·

I fay, let him a while give place,
For I will prove, a fiery face
Is to the owner no difgrace,
                Nor odious.

Who hath a fiery face, that man
Is faid to have a rich face, an
Rubies about his nofe, none can
                Deny it;

And all men know as well as I,
That what is rich, moft eagerly
We covet, and no coft deny
                To buy it.

Some have their cloathes fold from their back,
And fome their lands, and fome will lack
Meat, rather than good fherry, fack
                And claret.

And they fwear (and fwear truth) that thofe
Which drink fmall beer, and wear good cloathes,
Do offer wrong unto their nofe,
                And marr it.

If in Rome's fenate long-nos'd men
Were chofe for wifeft, tell me then,
Why thefe fhould not be praifed, when
                All men know,

A fiery face ne'er is without
A rich nofe : and how far a fnout
That's rich exceeds a long to doubt,
                Or call men to
                    Difpute

Difpute or to capitulate,
This matter's not fo intricate,
But any may expoftulate,

            And judge it :

And if judge truly he'll confefs,
Fire-rich, exceeds long wife, I guefs,
No man that hath true worthinefs

            Will grudge it.

Befides, the world knows this, that we
Affirm thofe gracious that we fee
But blufh, and call it modefty

            In people.

A rich face always blufhes, fo
It doth all faces elfe out go,
As far as St. Faith's is below

            Paul's fteeple.

He that reads this, and does not fay,
A fiery face hath won the day,
In judgment fhews himfelf a boy,

            And heedlefs.

Nor will I fpend more words to fhew,
What commendation men do owe
To Captain Jones his face, you know,

            'Tis needlefs.

E   To

To the R E A D E R.

R E A D E R, read on : here you may happ'ly
    meet
News, pleafing more, than what's cried in your
    ftreet.
Jones is reviv'd ; ne'er ftart ; the danger's paft ;
What he hath done long fince, now makes him laft.
His laft brave actions never fung before,
We offer to your view, nor write we more
Than he made good on oath : then, pray, believe
What here you'll find : thus by your faith he'll live.
Next, fpare your cenfure on his Poet's ftile ;
Had it gone high, his ghoft had kept a quoil
To be furmounted : down-right were his blows ;
Down-right his fpeech, down-right to's grave he
    goes.
Onely his fame by your opinion may
Make him ftill live, though now he's duft or clay.

The

The Wonderful and Surprizing

VOYAGES

OF

CAPTAIN JONES

To PATAGONIA.

PART II.

WILL nothing pleafe the tafte of thefe
    rough times,
But rue and wormwood ftuft in profe
    or rhimes?
No verfe to make our Poet's Laureate,
But fmart Iambicks lafhing King or State?
Muft all turn Mercuries, thefe times to fit,
By poifoning Fame with their quick-filver wit?
That name that's got by fome notorious ill,
And merit gives, is hateful to our quill.
But if the laft brave acts of Captain Jones,
Which can move mirth and fear, and break no bones,
May be admitted in this ruffling age,
Behold him here re-mounted on our ftage.
Yet know we ftill are ty'd to our low ftrain;
We muft not once tranfcend his down-right vein.

And

And if you meet ought favouring of a lye,
(Reader believe't) 'tis Jones that ſpeaks, not I.
We left him priz'd on Change, too dear 'twas
    thought,
* Twenty-four Dons, and all not worth a groat,
Compar'd to him, though each had had command
Over great armies, preſs'd for ſea and land.
Here ſee him ſhipp'd for his dear native coaſt ;
Where e'er he comes you'll find he'll rule the roaſt,
With new found foes, who attempt his force to
    ſhake ;
But ſleeping lions 'tis not wiſe to wake.
Now once more Neptune doth his waves inlarge,
Swoln big with pride, that fate had giv'n him charge,
And weighty convoy of this mighty man
To whence he came : but ere the ſhip had ran
Ten glaſſes out, comes Boreas with a cloud
As black as ink ; the ſteers-man cries aloud,
Down with the top-ſail, keep the ſprit-ſail tight,
Hail the main bowling. Whilſt this maſk of light,
Uſher'd with light'ning plows the angry deep,
High as her ſelf in ridges, and as ſteep
As Cair's † tall pyramids : the labouring ſhip,
Like a chaf'd bear with maſtives, ſtrives to keep
Her beak aloft ; ſome billows ſhe breaks through,
Others mount over her at poop and prow..
Jones heard this ſtir unmov'd : from Neptune ſtill
He hop'd no good, nor ever fear'd his ill.
Thus whilſt the careful ſea-men work and pray,
He careleſs, to his cabin calls his boy,
And makes him read to him the ancient ſtories
Of our old Engliſh worthies, and their glories ;
How our St. George did the fell dragon gore ;
The like atchievement of Sir Eglemore :
Topas ‡ hard queſt after th' elf-queen to Berwicke :
St. Bevis cow, and Guy's fierce boar of Warwick.

    * Twenty-four Spaniſh commanders given in exchange for him.
    † Large mountains in Wales.
    ‡ Sir Topas, rhime in Chaucer.

Theſe

These stories read, exalt his haughty mind,
Above the servile fear of sea or wind;
The ship's hard state grew now from ill to worse;
Between two hideous seas acrofs her courfe,
Her whole bulk groans; her beak and main-maft
  break.
Shook with this fhock, fhe fprings a dangerous leak:
Which her fly foe foon finds, and to begin
Like a dire dropfy, drenches all within.
Thus whilft a treacherous in-mate fills her womb,
She's forc'd to be her own deftructions tomb.
And overburthen'd with what bore her before,
She's down-right founder'd, and can work no more.
Here might be feen the fad effects of fear,
Which feveral ways in feveral men appear:
Some cry'd, fome pray'd, whilft others fwear or rave,
To leave the land to make the fea their grave.
Jones fwoln with the brave actions of his knights,
Big as the fea, afcends and Neptune cites
To fingle combat: when a boifterous wave,
Which Neptune fent to make him Neptune's flave,
Whirls him a cable's length to fea, the fhip
Sinks with the reft, who give this world the flip.
Well now, Sir Jones, 'tis time to fhew your fkill;
You muft fwim ftoutly for't, or drink your fill.
No danger frights thee, thou brave man of merit,
Thy body is buoy'd up by thy blow'n fpirit.
As a grim * fea-calf ftill prefaging ftorms,
Wallows and wantons in cold Thetis arms:
Juft fuch is Jones: as if he had been bred,
With her finn'd fry within her watry bed.
No fhip for help, no land for hope appears;
Horror of billows roaring in his ears.
Nothing fupports but confidence alone, as
If fome prefs'd whale muft take up Jones like Jonas.
At laft (alas!) he finds he is no fifh,
His fpirit 'gins to leave his treacherous flefh.

 * Always portending ftorms when they are feen to play.

Con-

Continual labouring makes his limbs wax ftark
And ftiff with cold, his optic fenfe grows dark ;
Neptune infults, and brandifhing his mace,
Makes his rude billows dafh him o'er the face.
Now fee the fate of noble refolution,
When Jones thought nothing but of diffolution,
Man's conftant friend a gentle Dolphin * glides
Between his thighs, on whom he mounts, and rides
In poft with mighty fpeed, through wind and
    weather ;
So his kind fifh holds out he cares not whither ;
Like a bold centaur bravely he curvets
From ridge to ridge ; 'twas ftrange, how faft he fits
In this rough road ; but Jones learn'd from his
    cradle
To ride without a ftirrup or a faddle ;
When on the mountain's tops wild mares he 'fpied,
He fuck'd them dry, and then ftraight up and ride.
At laft at this high fpeed he gets the fight
Of land, fo near, he's ready to alight,
When his kind fifh much griev'd to leave the bur-
    then
She lov'd fo well, to fea again doth turn
With mighty fpeed, ftill Jones doth her beftride,
Believing now he fhould to th' India's ride.
Fain would he turn her, but he knew not how,
He never knew a bridle's want till now :
At laft the faithful fifh preferring higher,
Her rider's fafety than her own defire,
She turns her courfe about with happy hafte,
And fo our errant knight on land fhe caft.
Some Spanifh writers flatly do deny
He fuffer'd wreck, and plainly term't a lye :
They fay the fhip that led this dangerous dance,
Was built by Lewis, King Henry's fon of France,

---

* The Dolphin is always obferved to be a lover of man.

And

And took that name from him, who bears that
    name *,
As eldeſt ſon, who ſtill is ſtil'd the ſame :
They write Jones got this ground t' augment his
    glory,
And cheat the world with this ſtupendious ſtory ;
But let the reader judge if this be true,
And know pale envy ſtill doth worth purſue.
Well now to Jones again, we may conceive,
He was not ill apaid to take his leave
Of this rough element : nor did account it
Much worſe to go on foot, than ride ſo mounted.
'Tis true, he rode this lofty fiſh in ſtate,
But 'twas too near the boiſterous fit of fate ;
He fear'd not fortune nor her wheel, tho' fickle,
Yet loth he was to be laid up in pickle ;
Or that his manly limbs ſhould be a feaſt
For ſharks, or crabs, or congers to digeſt.
His next work is to find ſome habitation,
Tho' he came ſafely there, 'twas in mean faſhion,
The ſelf-ſame cloathes which when Alonſo brav'd
    him,
He made him wear, and to the galley ſlav'd him.
And tho' this laſt foul ſtorm had little harm'd him,
It ſeem'd to ſome ſtrange thing to have transform'd
    him
Rigid and rough, long wet and felter'd locks,
Like Babel's King, when turn'd into an ox † :
For a freſh-water ſoldier none could doubt him,
The ſea's ſalt tears ran trickling round about him.
In this cold plight he leaves the beachy ſtrand,
And coaſts the main with many a weary ſtand.
At laſt he ſpies a houſe, not great, but good ;
For here he finds a brother of his brood,
Who had adventur'd in thoſe ways before,
And rais'd ſome fortune by't, and gave it o'er.

* The eldeſt ſon of the King of France always ſtiled the
Dolphin.
† Nebuchadnezzar.

He quickly finds that Jones had 'scap'd some wreck;
Experience, charity, and pity speak
On this behalf; the good man bids him in,
And, with Y'are kindly welcome, doth begin.
He spoke in Dutch, which gladded Jones, for he
Could speak as well as * *Grace dw worth awbee.*
Which language a Dutch pilot well had taught him,
When Greenfield to America had brought him.
By this, the Stove's made ready, in goes Jones;
Dries his wet garments, comforts nerves and bones.
The table's set with homely wholesome cheer,
And to make all compleat, strong Lubeck beer.
A Dutch froe was his mate, more fat than fair,
But wond'rous free, and there to debonair.
Which made Jones ask, What country 'twas that
    gave,
This noble welcome to her humble slave?
He's answer'd, 'Tis the Netherlands, the States
Brave seat of war, where many broken pates
Are got and given, and for his wants supply,
The good strong town of Flushing stood fast by,
Where Sir John Norris did command in chief,
For England's glory and the State's relief.
This tickled Jones with joy; for Horace Vere,
Norris, and he had been (I know not where)
Comrades in arms, ere Jones did entertain,
That cross design with Cumberland for Spain.
But now a bed does well, to take some rest,
Where this good host directs his weary guest.
And having slept his fill, he timely rose,
Takes a most thankful leave, and on he goes.
His purpose is to take his passage over
At the next port he finds; from thence to Dover.
But first at Flushing he resolves to touch,
Where his old friend, the bulwark of the Dutch,
Brave Norris holds his troop; here Jones arrives,
Just as he came from goal, except his gives,

___
* The same in Welch.

Clad

Clad in his flavish robe of friars grey,
His cap true blue ; no company, but they
That will not leave him whilst he hath a rag,
Such as possess the beggar with his bag.
Winds, storms, nor seas, nor ought that could undo
　　him,
Could make them flinch, like friends they stick
　　close to him.
And thus accompanied he doth approach
To th'General's house, neither with steed nor coach ;
But in his manly foot-march : 'twas the time,
When Norris with his chiefs were set to dine.
Jones presseth to the parlour from the hall,
And there accosts the noble General.
Who ey'd him quickly, and cries out (O fate !)
Live I to see the strength of England's state ?
Breath'st thou brave man at arms ? Jones art thou
　　he ?
Or is it Mars himself disguis'd like thee ?
Quoth Jones, The scourge of Spaniards and of Spain,
Whom they have felt and foil'd, but to their pain,
Stands here ; and yet would breathe some few years
　　longer,
To prove King Philip or myself the stronger.
The rest was dear embraces, and his place
By Norris' side ; and then a hasty grace.
Now might I dwell upon the luscious cheer,
Which here grew cold, whilst each man's eye and
　　ear
Fed on the person and discourse of Jones,
And quite forgot their toasts and marrow-bones.
And whilst his strange adventures past, he tells ;
The Captains, Serjeant-Majors, Colonels,
Fast to admire him, and are fill'd with wonder,
And feel no hunger tho' their bellies thunder.
Here mark his constancy, beyond these men,
He eats and talks, and eats and talks again.

　　　　　F　　　　　　Their

Their maws are cloy'd to hear those deeds of his,
His stories are his meal's parenthesis.
But when he spoke of Spain, 'tis past belief,
What fearful wounds he gave the chine of beef.
A capon garnish'd with slic'd lemons stood
Before him, which he tore as he were wood ;
And made it legless ere he made a pause,
Merely in malice to the Spanish sauce.
He wrecks his wrath on ev'ry dish that's nigh him,
And spoil'd a custard that stood trembling by him ;
Grown pikes and carps, and many a dainty dish,
That far excell'd his tame Crotonian fish.
At last his fury 'gan to be assuag'd,
And then the General all his friends engag'd,
To give him soldier's welcome in a rowse
Of lusty rhenish, till both men and house
Turn round.   Once two great deities conjoin'd
To work his fall, with hideous seas and wind :
Now only Bacchus takes the man to task ;
And lays sore to him with his potent cask.
And whilst with lusty grape o'er-borne Jones reels,
H' assaults his head, and so trips up his heels.
But up he rose again with vigour stout,
And swears, tho' foil'd, he'll try another bout.
They all were now high flown, when colonel Skink,
Fills a huge bowl of sherry sack, to drink
A health to England's Queen, and Jones is he
Must take't in pledge ; and so he did : but see
The strange antipathy between this man
And Spanish grape as well as Spanish Don.
Against them both his stomach fierce doth rise,
No sooner drank but up again it flies.
This odd distemper made him half asham'd,
But there's no help, he was with wrath inflam'd ;
Nor was he pleas'd with Skink of this affront,
(For so he took't) he knew Skink could not want
The wine of Rhene for healths :- why then in sack,
Unless it were to lay him on his back ?

                                                Fir'd

Fir'd with this thought, he catch'd at his buff-coat,
Then grapples clofe ; and had pluck'd out his throat,
But that the wary General interpofes
His hands and friends between their bloody nofes :
And with ftrong reafons, fmiles, and fmooth allays,
He damps the fury of thefe fiery boys,
And left them (as he thought) well reconcil'd,
But by th' effect he found he was beguil'd.
The night difpers'd them now to feveral ways,
As they were quarter'd. Jones with Norris ftays,
Who fent him the next morn a brave rich fuit,
Intended for himfelf, with all things to't.
Scant was he drefs'd, when Skink unto him fends
A Captain, boldly to demand amends
For laft night's work, and Jones, to do him right,
A bullet muft exchange in fingle fight.
For which himfelf and fecond would not mifs,
Where Jones defign'd to meet with him and his.
This Jones accepts, and fwears before that night
He fhall hear from him, how and where he'll fight.
He thus difpatch'd, Sir Roger Williams enters,
To whom much kind difcourfe paft o'er ; he ventures
To tell his difference with Skink ; which told,
Sir Roger like a Britain true and bold,
Protefts himfelf his fecond, haftes to Skink,
Tells him, h' need fight well, as well as drink :
That Jones and he at the South-poftern gate,
Early next morn would meet him and his mate,
With fword and piftol hors'd, and there agree,
To fight it two to two, or Jones and he.
Then comes to Jones, fupply'd him with a horfe
Well rid and fierce ; Bucquoy had felt his force
Before Breda ; then gives that fword and belt,
Which Prince * Llwellin wore, when flain near
     Bealt.

---

* The prince of South Wales, who was flain near Beal:,
a town in Brecknockfhire.

The

The hour come, thefe champions foon appear,
They fpend no time in words; in full career,
Jones charges bravely clofe up to his breaft,
And fires, but fortune turn'd it to the beft:
Makes him thro' hafte forget to prime his pan,
So mifs'd his fhot, and fo preferv'd the man.
Vex'd with this fail, he flings with all his might,
Worfe than the bullet, had his hand gone right,
His piftol at his face; 'twas aim'd fo near,
It raz'd his cheek, and took quite off his ear.
Skink's bullet pierc'd the blow of Jones his faddle,
And flightly circumcis'd his foreman's noddle;
The feconds ftood attending the event
Of this firft charge, both refolutely bent,
If either in th' encounter had been fped,
To run the fame adventure they both did.
But when they faw the bravery of their fight,
Both having loft their blood, the quarrel flight:
They both deteft fuch men fhould be deftroy'd,
By which their country fhould be fore annoy'd:
With joint confent their power they unite
To ride up to them, and break off the fight:
Thus got between them, all beft means they ufe
To take it up: which both enrag'd refufe.
They urge the equal terms on which they ftood,
In point of honour: both had loft their blood,
Both fought it well; how light their quarrel's ground,
Not worth one drop of blood, much lefs a wound.
Then bid them look on their dear country's woe,
Whofe breafts muft fuffer for the ill they do.
Reafon takes place of wrath, they both accord,
And mifchief's engine refts; they fheath the fword.
And thus (in few) this dangerous duel ends,
Fierce foes they met, and now return good friends:
Their furgeons ftanch their blood, for yet they bled,
And clap a cap on Jones his nether head.
This news comes quickly to the General's ear,
Who when he heard their lives were out of fear,

He

He gently chides them that they would expofe,
Their limbs unto the various chance of blows
In fingle duel, when the common good,
No longer ftands than fuch good members ftood.
Ten days are fpent ere Jones could ftand upright,
Thro' his flight hurt: which come, the noble knight
Brave Norris he takes leave of, with the reft
Of that brave martial crew, and then addreft
Himfelf for England : Joy thou happy Ifle,
Thy fon returns that hath kept all this quoil ;
Ye bluftering boys of Britain feaft and quaff all ;
The man's at hand whofe prefence makes you laugh
   all.
Welcome to Dover, thou great fon of Mavors,
So fpeak the mayor of Dover on his grave horfe,
Mounted to meet him with his reverend train,
All gown, who cry him welcome home from Spain.
After fome fhort repaft, on poft he rides
To Non-fuch, where her Majefty refides,
Where he was foon brought up to kifs her hand,
By his dear friend George earl of Cumberland.
But then when took to private conference,
What news of moment, what intelligence,
What Spanifh plots, what myfteries of ftate,
Unto her Majefty he did relate,
'Twas wrapp'd in clouds too high for me to know it ;
Then pardon, reader, that I do not fhew it.
But 'twas obferv'd he gave a written book
Unto her hand : on which fhe deign'd to look,
And feem'd to flight it in the public face
Of court ; yet made fome ufe of 't in a place
That's privy, fo difmifs'd him to his reft,
Or her court's welcome ; as to him feem'd beft.
'Twas now the time when * Effex was engag'd
In Ireland 'gainft Tyrone, with whom he wag'd
A bloody war : which to the Queen and ftate
Seem'd long and coftly : after much debate

     * Robert, earl of Effex.

It is refolv'd to pick out fuch a man,
Whofe active force and fpirit dares and can
Put a full period to this war at once,
Without delay, and this was Captain Jones,
On whom they pitch, who fed on hopes in vain,
To get fome fmall command to conquer Spain.
'Tis firft refolv'd he muft reduce Tyrone,
'Till that be done he muft let Spain alone.
Thus his commiffion's feal'd to raife his force,
A compleat regiment of Britifh horfe:
He's thence to waft them o'er the Irifh brine;
And then his force with noble Effex join.
Jones loft no time, goes in five days to Wales:
Shews his commiffion, tells them glorious tales;
He need not beat a drum, nor found his trumpet,
His name's enough to make thefe Britons jump at
This brave employment under fuch a chief,
Whofe fame's referve enough for their relief.
Perplex'd he was in chufing his commanders,
For he ftill fancied beft his old Highlanders;
But many worthies of the lower parts,
Offer to him their fortunes and their hearts.
But all refpects put by, h' enlifteth ten
Of his old gang, all hard-bred mountain-men,
For his life-guard, Thomas Da Price a Pew,
Jenkin Da Prichard, Evan David Hugh,
John ap John Jenkin, Richard John dap Reefe,
And Tom Dee Bacgh, a fierce rat at green cheefe,
Llewelling Reefe ap David, Watkin Jenkin,
With Howell Reefe ap Robert, and young Philkin;
Thefe for his guard, his officers in chief,
Lieutenant colonel Craddock, a ftout thief,
With major Howell ap Howell of Pen Crag,
Well known for plund'ring many cow and nag;
Captain Pen Vaure, a branch of Tom John Catty,
Whofe word in's colours was, YE ROGUES have
    at ye.

                                        Griffith

Griffith ap Reefe ap Howell ap Coh ap Gwillin,
Reefe David Shone ap Ruthero ap William ;
With many more, whofe names 'twere long to write,
The reft their acts will get them names in fight.
We muft conceive they all were men of fame,
For here we fee them all men of great name.
Jones with thefe blades advanceth to the * dale,
There lines himfelf and them with noble ale,
Of fuch antiquity as hath not been there,
The like fince † Robert of the vale was feen there,
Who us'd to fink thofe kilderkins of merit,
To raife the heat of his prophetic fpirit.
His forces flipp'd, at iaft on board he goes,
A lufty fouth-eaft gale fo fairly blows,
That forty hours eafily brought him in,
To Dublin harbour where he lands his men ;
There getting knowledge where the army lay,
To the Lord General he takes his way ;
From whom a noble welcome he receives,
And good frefh quarter to his troops he gives.
Jones firft informs himfelf in what condition
Tyrone's made up for war, what ammunition.
How fortify'd in camp, what force, what watch,
How victuall'd, all occafion he doth catch
To take him tripping ; when at length he found,
He would not give nor take an equal ground,
To hazard battle, he refolves to try him,
In fuch a way as he fhould not deny him,
Unlefs with lofs of honour ; he indites
This fearful challenge which his 'fquire writes :
Falfe traitor to thy country and thy Queen,
I, he who yet my peer have never feen,
In feats of arms, whofe martial hand hath flain
Kings with their armies, half unpeopled Spain :

* A little village by Milford.
† An old Welch prophet, who foretold the landing of
Henry the feventh there.

f.   Done

Done more than I can write; I say, I he
Urge thee to single duel: and to thee
Give thee free choice of weapon, time, and place,
On foot or horse-back: think it no disgrace,
That I a private Captain, thou a chief,
(My deeds make me admir'd, thee thine a thief)
Call thee to question, 'twere ambition
In thee, to hope to fall by such a one,
T' augment my praise I wish thee five times stronger,
Live till I meet thee, and but little longer.
This done, a herald is straight charged with it,
In public to Tyrone's own hand to give it,
Who to him hastes, and in the public view
Of all his army says, (Tyrone) to you,
I have command to bring from Captain Jones
This challenge; read it, and resolve at once.
He takes it, reads it, and admires the man,
That sends him this high brave, who if he can
But half he writes, he counts himself but lost,
To meet him; yet in sight of all his host
This brave was given him : thus his honour lyes
At stake, and therefore desperately replies.
Tell your brave man I am not conquer'd yet,
Nor can by words but blows, he shall be met,
Before to-morrow noon, on yon green plot,
Surrounded with the bog, neither with shot,
Nor head-steel'd dart : this sword I wear shall do't,
Arm'd cap-a-pee, no horse, but foot to foot.
He thus dispatch'd, Tyrone doth straight seek out,
Brain Mac-kill cow, a strong sturdy lout,
Made up with nerves, and brawn and bone so mighty,
He felt no burthen were it ne'er so weighty.
The strongest man in all his camp by half.
Milo's great bull to him was but a calf,
Bred in the Irish wilds 'mongst bogs and woods,
And like an outlaw liv'd on other's goods.
And this is he on whom Tyrone now fixt,
To personate himself in fight betwixt

Him and our Jones, true arms of largeſt ſize,
He puts on him, then to his loins he ties
Morglay his truſty ſword, then ſwears devoutly,
If in this combat he behave him ſtoutly,
He'll raiſe his means above two Engliſh Barons,
In lands and ſheep and cows and luſty garrons:
Bryan's all confidence and haſtens thither,
Where Jones and he muſt try their force together.
The place deſign'd was hardly twelve yards ſquare,
No traverſing of ground, no boys play there,
The reſt was bog, o'er which ſome planks were laid
To paſs them o'er ; and then to ſtop all aid,
Were took from thence : here Jones our vailant
    fighter
Advanceth firſt: Bryan with his fell ſimiter
Is hard at hand ; they ſpare no time for words,
Their mettle is the whetſtone of their ſwords.
They clap together like two ſons of thunder,
Their blades ſtruck light'ning, whilſt the earth
    quak'd under
The burthen ſhe bore ; no ſtroke that's given, but
    death
Seems to attend it, till both out of breath
Conſent to make a ſtand ; but this ſhort reſt,
Was like a ſallad with a mutton's breaſt
To their ſharp ſtomachs, to't they go again,
And lay on load like devils, not like men.
Their well-try'd arms do bluſh with their own
    blood,
To find their fleſh in whoſe defence they ſtood,
Stand, whilſt it fell: for that their keen ſwords whipt
    off,
As if they would each other make a chipt loaf.
At laſt, as I have ſeen a man of war
Exalt a Carrick, which exceeds him far,
In bulk and ſtrength : ſo Jones deals now with
    Bryan,
With ſhuns and ſhifts, more like a Fox than Lion.

For

For (to speak truly) this fell Pagan lout,
Doth so belabour Jones from head to foot,
That both his ears do oft with sorrow sing,
And's eyes see stars at noon (a wond'rous thing)
We must conceive those furious blows he dealt,
Were well repaid with use, which Bryan felt.
But Jones esteeming it an equal thing
To be self-conquer'd, and long conquering,
Resolves to put the business out of doubt
With one pass more, which was the fatal bout.
On this resolve, with both his hands he press'd,
The pummel of his sword against his breast,
Then like a thunder-bolt tilts swiftly at him:
With th' fear of this, Bryan had quite forgot him.
That 'twas a bog behind, so backward springs,
And his whole body up to the arm-pits flings, .
Amidst the bog. Jones, driven with his own force,
Missing his thrust falls headlong in the gorse,
But pitch'd upon his foe, by happy fate,
With which o'er-borne, our Jones so mauls his pate,
That th' helmet flies, and leaves his head to th'
        danger,
Of being the anvil of our Jones his anger:
And now the day is his, his strength he strains,
With hand and hilt to beat out Bryan's brains:
Who cries out quarter, Man of Mars I yield
My self and sword, the honour of the field.
And where the power rests, 'tis much better far,
To give than take a life in chance of war.
This and the bog doth cool the wrath of Jones,
He spares his life and draws him forth at once.
Besides he scorn'd posterity should tell,
That by his hand Tyrone so nobly fell.
And thus O'Neal his captive (as he thought)
In this foul plight unto the camp he brought:
Presents him to the General, and then speak,
Sir, if you have ten more Tyrones to take,
                    Command,

Command, I'll do't ; here fee him hither led
By me, who all this charge and ftir hath bred.
The joy was great, but fhort ; 'twas quickly known,
This was but fome impoftor for Tyrone :
And this an Irifh captive at firft view
Made known, who him and his condition knew.
This bred a qualm in fome, whil'ft others fmil'd,
To fee their Britifh champions fo beguil'd,
And that Tyrone had bobb'd him with this jeer,
To match his cow-herd with our mountaineer.
Jones vex'd with this, retires unto his tent,
An angry, dirty, defperate, malecontent.
Three days thus fpent, his wrath no longer bears
This bafe affront ; (like Scævola *,) he fwears
He'll kill Tyrone in 'midft of all his force,
Tho' in the act himfelf be made a corfe :
In this wild mood by night he doth convey
Himfelf, where he fuppos'd the rebel lay :
Who wifely rais'd his camp the day before,
March'd far thro' defart woods, and would no more
Of thefe affronts ; which to put off agen,
Might breed contempt of him with his own men.
Two days Jones fpends in quefts to find him out ;
At laft he was encounter'd with a rout
Of ravening wolves, who fiercely all at once,
Affail'd the back and face of manly Jones.
'Twas time to draw, elfe thefe wild Irifh dogs,
Had been fo bold to fhake him by the logs :
But when his fword was out he makes them feel,
Their teeth are not fo fharp as his true fteel.
The firft good blow he dealt took off a head,
The fecond made one two : the next he fped,
With a fore thruft at mouth, and out at tail :
A fourth which his pofteriors doth affail,
With his ftrong heel he hurls againft a tree,
Twelve paces from his kick, and there lies he :

* Scævola againft Porfenna in Livy.

His fword rips out another's empty paunch ;
The next limps off from him with half a haunch.
We muft conceive 'twas time to lay about him,
For here were thofe that fought to eat, not rout him.
Nor 'fcap'd he free, the rich fword fcarf he wore
About his loins, they all to fitters tore.
His boots pluck'd off by bits, fome flefh to boot,
No quarter free from fcars from head to foot.
And (to conclude) from thefe wild Irifh witches *,
He 'fcapes fcant with a hand's breadth of his breeches.
Wearied with blows and kicks, at laft they fly him,
And take a fnarling leave as they go by him.
Thus Jones, half worried, haftes unto the camp.
There's none could fay the cloathes he wore were
    damp
With night perdues, unlefs they meant to flout him ;
For (to fpeak truth) he had no cloathes about him.
Thus come, he fwears by the immortal powers,
He had maintain'd a battle full five hours,
With forty duels, five and twenty kill'd,
Routed the reft ; who had all took the field
'Gainft him alone ; all rais'd with him to fight,
To his deftruction, or t' eclipfe his might,
By that old timorous treacherous kern Tyrone,
Who durft as well meet death as him alone.
The plight our Jones appear'd in, made none doubt,
But he had had at leaft a devilifh bout,
If not with devils ; on him each man feeth,
The fearful character of nails and teeth.
We may not ftand to fhew what Effex' fenfe
Was on thefe actions, nor the confequence
They did import : the progrefs of this ftory,
Haftens our Mufe to Jones his farther glory.
Fame thefe atchievements brings to England's ftate ;
Which held the Queen and council in debate

    * Lupanthropos, witches that take the fhapes of wolves
upon them in Ireland.

About

About this man ; and all at laſt ſuppos'd,
In policy he's not to be expos'd,
To the cloſe dang'rous plots of ſuch a foe,
Who neither values faith nor honour, ſo
His miſchiefs take ſucceſs : and thus the ſtate
Loſe this dear limb, and then repent too late.
Some looking deeper into Jones his ſpirit,
Knowing he knew too much of his own merit,
Hold it not ſafe he ſhould be open to,
The windy baits of that ſo ſubtile foe,
To gain him to his part ; whoſe haughty mind
Would ſoon take fire ; then could not be confin'd.
And if by ſuch a plot they ſhould be croſs'd,
They all conclude that kingdom were but loſt.
Theſe grounds invite them wholly to decline
His warfare there ; ſo on ſome grand deſign
Pretended they invite his quick repair,
To England's court to act this great affair.
He comes, but leaves his Britiſh troops to fight:
Tyrone to death ; whoſe acts who pleaſe to write,
May meet with ſubjects brave to rant upon,
But for myſelf I am quite tir'd with one.
And thus tranſported from the Iriſh ſtrands,
At Aberuſt * with a Welch port he lands ;
Where ere two days he fully ſpent for reſt,
A goodly veſſel, with croſs winds oppreſs'd,
Comes boiling in ; Jones by her colours knows
She is of Spain : his colour comes and goes
At ſight of her's ; that ſuch a godly prey,
Should come (as 'twere) to meet him in his way.
He muſters ſtraight a troop of Britiſh lads,
Who on their mountain geldings clap their pads ;
With ruſty bills inſtead of ſtaves in reſt ;
Such were their horſe, ſuch were their arms at beſt.
Then with a fowling-piece the ſhip they hail,
With confidence that ſhe would ſtraight ſtrike ſail ;

* A Town and Port in the County of Cardigan.

But

But fhe makes anfwer, that fhe was too hot,
From her broadfide with twenty culverin fhot.
This ftruck a ftand, till Jones cry'd out, what doubt
    ye ?
The day is ours, mafters lay about ye ;
Lead the forlorn up bravely, and be bold,
I'll bring the rear, for they know me of old ;
If once my name or perfon they defcry,
My life for yours they'll either yield or fly.
Made bold with this, in full career they ride,
Up to the ridges of the flowing tide.
But when they came breaft-high amongft the waves,
Their horfe more wife by half then thefe mad knaves,
Snort at the foaming billows, turn their tails,
And make a fair retreat from fea and fails ;
Which, left it fhould feem done on terms of fear,
Jones to the front, now haftens from the rear,
And leads them back again in good array,
Neither with hafty flight, nor much delay.
At his return he fearcheth all that coaft,
To find a herring-boat or two at moft ;
With which he doubts not but he'll fink or take
This lufty fhip : whofe braveft men will quake
To hear his name.   But fate that had decreed
To fave her, caus'd her hoyfe her fails with fpeed :
So with a ftrong fore-wind away fhe flies,
And leaves our Jones to feek fome other prize.
Thus crofs'd in this defign to court he went,
Where he is met with noble compliment ;
And from the Queen fuch grace he doth receive,
As he deferv'd, and ftood with her to give.
Now for the great affair that call'd him back,
The Lords muft pump for't in a cup of fack
To help invention : Jones muft be prefer'd
To fome employment, be it ne'er fo hard.
In deep confult and long difcourfe they fat on't,
And ftudied for't ; at laft they lighted pat on't.
                        It

It is refolv'd, that he muft be the man,
To go in embaffy to Prefter John.
The bufinefs carried with't a glorious face ;
Employ'd Ambaffador unto his Grace.
The dangerous voyage to a place remote,
Affects him moft to get his name more note
In foreign Lands ; he'll not refufe the work,
Were't to the Great Mogul, or the Great Turk.
A lufty fhip's prepar'd, again he goes ;
But what this great employment was, who knows ?
Reader, I know thy thoughts are ftrongly bent
To know this firft defign, on which he went.
But know this firft, that Prince's fecret ways,
Are fuch as fhips cut thorough deepeft feas,
Which fhut ftill as they ope, and him that founds,
And enters too far in, their deepnefs drowns.
If bare conjectures may give light to thee,
Here take them freely ; harmlefs thoughts are free.
Perhaps this high blown fpirit now is fent
To foreign air, where it may purge and vent,
And fo return more fit the ftate to ferve
In their commands, who yet muft him obferve.
Perhaps he went this prieftly Prince to gain
Unto our church ; who gave good proof in Spain
Of's power in this ; or to negotiate,
Commerce between the Æthiop and our ftate,
For tufks of Elephants to haft our knives,
Apes and baboons and pugs to pleafe our wives ;
Which things fatiety makes common there,
And curiofity o'erprizeth here.
Be't what it will, our Jones is gone upon't,
And we may know he will make fomething on't.
His treacherous friend the fea his charge receives,
And with fome flattering gales his hopes deceives,
Making the Land his firmer friend appear
Still lefs ; until at laft it brought him where
He loft her fight : for three month's time he makes
Good way ; at laft the wind his wings forfakes,

The

The ſhip's becalm'd, and to the Port ſhe ſeeks,
She gains not half a league for thirteen weeks.
Jones find this lazy war offends him more,
Than all thoſe hideous ſtorms out-rid before.
Theſe ſad effects this ſleepy calm attend ;
Victual and beverage ſpent ; leſs hope of end:
Then fear of further miſeries enſues,
The ſea with calms his patience doth abuſe,
Turns deviliſh ſtateſman, puts on a ſmooth face,
Salutes and kills them with a ſoft embrace.
'Twas now far worſe with Jones than erſt with Skink ;
For three weeks his own urine is his drink,
Which his hot body had ſo oft ſublim'd ;
'Tis grown a cordial, like gold thrice calcin'd.
Breezes of wind at laſt his ſails diſplay,
And waft him into the Barbarick bay ;
Then to the Arabick, next the pilot laves,
His boiſterous charge in *Mare rubrum*'s waves.
And laſtly he attains, beyond all hope,
Errocco, the ſole Port of Æthiope ;
And here he lands, and empties many a bowl,
To allay the fury of his thirty ſoul.
After ſome reſt he gets intelligence,
Where 'twas the Prince then kept his reſidence ;
Where he repairs, and's told when he comes thither,
The Prince and town are both remov'd together
Some ten miles off. The Prince and town ! (quoth
　　　Jones)
I have met my match : here's people make no bones
Of things beyond belief. And yet 'twas true ;
This town was tents which fifty thouſand drew,
And rais'd in th' inſtant, whereſoe'er the Prince
Sat down to ſport, or ſhew magnificence.
By Mount Amara now his court he rears ;
A mount far differing from the name it bears * :

---

* Read Purchas, in his relations of Æthiopia, touching
this mount.

If

If Paradife had e'er a fecond birth
Below the feat of faints, 'tis there on earth.
An humble valley is the garden where
This Mount is rais'd ; a vale fo rich, fo rare ;
Nature grew bankrupt drawing this rich plot,
And ftriving to be quaint, fhe quite forgot
To keep referves ; for by this work we know,
She made it fuch fhe could make no more fo.
Amidft this vale is rais'd this lofty ftructure,
Five leagues upright. It's outfides architecture
Unpolifh'd marble ; but fo rich, fo fair,
You'd think't a pillar of one ftone in th' air ;
By fome high power unto Atlas given,
To eafe his fhoulders whil'ft it proppeth heaven.
This goodly Mount a fpacious plain doth crown,
Imboft with Nature's gems, a velvet down
That's always green ; no froft, no winter here,
Continual fpring ; here Phœbus all the year,
From rife to fet, doth always fire his eye,
As loath to put fo fair an object by.
Here grow thofe happy trees from whence there
     fprings
That precious oil, which erft anointed Kings,
And facred priefts. Nor croud they here to take
One fenfe alone ; the fcent and fight partake.
So are they rank'd, as well to give a grace,
As fweet perfumes, for tribute to the place.
No orchard here, nor garden but the plain ;
The choiceft fruit all Europe doth contain,
Grow here unplanted, here's the lufcious grape,
That makes Jove's nectar : 'twas not Helen's rape
That ruin'd Troy : the apple * got from thence,
Had worth enough to do't. Here every fenfe
Would furfeit, but each object's rarity,
Gives appetite without fatiety ;

---

* The apple which three goddeffes, Juno, Pallas and Venus,
contended for, which was given by Paris to Venus ; where-
upon followed the deftruction of Troy.

Rofes

Rofes and tulips Flora gathers here,
When we have none, to crown her golden hair ;
And here Medea pick'd (if Jones fpeak truth)
Thofe herbs which turned antiquity to youth :
The only Phœnix deigns to weather here,
The only place like her without a peer :
Left all thefe fweets fhould want fweet harmony,
A numerous choir of nightingale's comply,
To warble forth the fweet Amara's praife,
Who turns their mourning notes to merry lays.
Amidft this plain there glides a filver brook,
So gently, that the fubtleft eye may look,
And find no motion ; on his violet banks
Thick Cyprus trees marfhal themfelves in ranks,
To keep out Phœbus ; whofe enamour'd beams,
Peep thro' each little crink to view his ftreams :
His pavement azure gravel intermixt
With orient pearls, and diamonds betwixt,
Which as the air's foft breath his furface purls,
Vary their glofs, and twinkle through his curls ɩ
Like a fteel'd glafs prefenting to the eye,
The fpangled beauty of the ftarry fky.
Here Dolphins leave the fea to wanton ; here
Carps fince the deluge their grown bodies cheer,
Umbrana's too ; fuch had * Vitellius known,
A province fhould have gone to purchafe one ;
Such is Amara, fuch is Tempe field,
Elyfium on earth unparallel'd.
'Twas here this royal prieft now kept his court ;
A place well fuiting with his fame and port.
And here comes Jones, where having made's addrefs,
Letters of credence given at his accefs,
In Latin writ : in the fame tongue he gives
Jones gracious words, which language Jones con-
ceives
To be Arabic, for the Latin tongue
He ne'er endur'd to learn nor old nor young ;

* A great epicure, and Emperor of Rome.

But

But that's all one, there's no reply expected,
Unto a rich pavilion he's directed
By men of state, where he is well attended,
With all that's rich, and to his rest commended.
Some few days spent, and time for audience got,
When Prester John in royal state was sat;
Jones studying how t' express his eloquence,
In some strange language which might pose the
　　　　Prince,
Now trouls him forth a full mouth'd Welsh oration,
Boldly deliver'd as became his nation.
The plot prov'd right, for not one word of sense
Could be pick'd from't, which vex'd the learned
　　　　Prince.
His learned linguists are call'd in to hear,
Who might as well have stopp'd each others ear,
For ought they understood, and all protest,
It was the very language of the beast.
Jones hath his end, and then to make it known,
He had more tongues t'express himself than one;
In a new tone he speaks, not half so rich,
But better known, 'twas English; unto which
An English Factor is interpreter,
Between our Captain and John Presbyter;
His business takes effect (what ere it was)
And great expresses of respect do pass
To Jones from him, as one he thought most rich,
In unknown tongues express'd in his first speech,
And so admires him for he knows not what:
But Jones may thank his mother-tongue for that.
His business done, he's led for recreation,
To take the pleasures of that pleasant nation,
To mount Amara's top, the chiefest grace,
And perfect beauty of that Kingdom's face;
And finding his great heart was most inclin'd
To martial feats, all in one motion join'd
T' invite him to their desarts, where he might
• Make trial of his force in manly fight,

With their wild beasts, and promis'd him consorts,
All truly try'd t' assist him in those sports.
The motion takes, a brave accoutred horse,
And his own arms, he and's associate force
Advance to hunt; methinks I see them all,
Drawn to the life in canvas * 'gainst the wall,
In some mean house made for good-fellowship,
How fierce they look, how brave they prance and
    skip;
With hounds and horns, and bills and picks and
    glaves,
And spears and clubs, and many light-foot knaves:
In this brave equipage they march away,
To the known haunts where these wild creatures
    prey.
'Twas Jones his trick of old to ride alone:
In hard adventures he'll admit of none
To share with him, from them he steals aside,
And in the desart by himself doth ride.
Nor rode he long, till just against him stalks
A ramping lion, new come from his walks;
Jones draws, the furious beast with fiery eyes,
And bristled mane, against his bosom flies;
But his keen sword met full with his fore paws,
And whipp'd them off; and so he 'scap'd his claws.
Nor stay'd it there, but gave a cruel wound
To his left jaw, and fell'd him to the ground.
Then nimbly wheels about, and stepp'd aside,
Leaps from his horse, which to a tree he ty'd;
Then turns again, and with his sword falls to't,
To end this combat with him foot to foot;
The wounded beast with all his power doth hasten,
His fearful fangs in Jones his throat to fasten.
Whilst on's hin feet he assaults him bolt upright,
With left hand arm'd, Jones stuns with him the
    right;

* Painted cloths in inns and victualling-houses.

Strikes

Strikes both his hin legs off ; yet on his ftumps,
The noble beaft unconquered fiercely jumps;
Full at his face with open mouth, and there,
(For his grim face could raife in Jones no fear)
In fhoots the deadly blade, and out behind,
Where't makes a fecond vent for life's fhort wind ;
This thruft with right hand arm'd fo home was lent,
That hand and hilt quite thro' together went ;
Where taking hold of his ftrong ftern (for truth
He fwears) he drew't quite thro' his trunk this mouth.
Then with fine force (the like was never feen)
He ftrips his infide out, and's outfide in.
Thus tergiverft upon his fteed he flings him,
Then mounts himfelf, and to the court he brings
    him.
Never was royal beaft fo grofly jaded,
But 'twas his fate which could not be evaded ;
Unto the gallants of the court he fhews,
How hard th' adventure was, what thrufts, what
    blows ;
On every circumftance he doth dilate ;
Nor adds he much to truth, nor much doth bate :
For much he fpoke, the lion made it good,
With lofs of his four legs, and his beft blood.
This ftrange atchievement ftrikes them all with
    wonder,
'Twas never feen fince Greece's Alexander.
Lyfimachus, Lyfander, nor Perdiccas *,
Nor any of his chiefs, ere did the like as
Our Jones in this : 'Tis true, they write they kill'd,
In fingle fight fome few of thefe in field ;
But here's a force borne with a higher fail,
Tranftorting tail to head, and head to tail.
The Prince in words this high atchievement prais'd :
But inward fear and jealoufy it rais'd
Of our brave Queen, whofe fceptre doth command,
Such men whofe power no nation can withftand.

   * Read Quintus Curtius concerning thefe.

                               Jones

Jones might so far on his own strength presume, as
To seise his throne, as * Cortez Montezuma's
Had done before. These thoughts he oft revolves
With troubled mind, and so in fine resolves
To shift him thence : makes for his fair pretence,
Matter of high and hasty consequence,
To be with speed convey'd unto our Queen ;
Except herself it must by none be seen.
This past on Jones, who parts with high content,
Nobly presented with fair compliment,
Amongst the rest, a Parrot, that could speak
All tongues but Jones his own ; that had a beak
Of perfect coral, plum'd as white as snow :
This he accepts, and so to sea does go :
Where under sail such welcome he receives,
As one dire foe unto another gives.
With calms, and storms, and winds, all cross, that
        bear,
The ship quite off the course that she would steer.
Long time thus spent, into a bay he drives,
And at a port unknown at last arrives :
Where he beholds a glorious castle built
High on a cliff, whose walls pure gold, or gilt,
To him appear'd. Which object caus'd him land,
To know who did this princely seat command.
He's told it is the Queen of No-land's place,
The only relict of her royal race ;
A maiden Queen that here doth keep her court,
Where many Kings and Princes of high port
Make their address, and lose themselves in love,
To purchase her's, for not a man can move
Her heart to wed, tho' ne'er so great his state,
Or form exact, such was the will of fate.
Here, as he lands, a large canoe was sent,
To know from whence he was, and whither bent.

* A private Spanish commander, that took this great King
of Mexico with a handful of men.

In

In this a Dutchman came by happy fate,
Who could his language to the Queen tranflate.
This man he tells, as briefly as he can,
His voyage from his Queen to Prefter John :
How by crofs winds in his return he's blown,
And forc'd into this port to him unknown.
Jones is refolv'd to fee and to be feen
Of this great Princefs, that our virgin Queen
Might know when he returns what form, what port
This royal virgin carried in her court,
Thus like an errant knight all arm'd compleat,
He marcheth boldly to her palace gate,
All maffy polifh'd brafs ; at his firft ward,
Six milk-white Panthers fierce were chain'd for
    guard.
Thence thro' a large great fpacious court he paft,
And fo afcends twelve ivory fteps at laft,
With ebon columns, unto which were ty'd,
Twelve fharp kept Lions, who all yawned wide
When ftrangers do approach. Jones thro' them all
Is fafely guarded to a goodly hall.
From thence afcends to rooms of greater ftate,
And comes at laft where this Princefs royal fat
Upon a ftrange rich bed, not ftuff'd with down,
But clofely wrought, and like a bladder blown ;
Three Æthiops on each fide, to fan the air,
With Oftridge plumes perfum'd as rich as fair.
Her beauty could not boaft of white and red,
But jet-like black ; about her crifp curl'd head
And cheeks, there hang rich flaming ftones and
    pearls,
That pafs'd Mark Anthony's Egyptian girls.
In brief ; if Tufcan liv'd to limn the night
Sparkling with ftars, this were her picture right.
No fooner to her fight doth Jones appear ;
Than to her heart his piercing eyes fhot fire ;
Which Cupid blows and rais'd into a flame,
That warms her zeal to invocate his name.

No part of Jones but in her eye exceeds
All human shape; some god he must be needs.
But when at her request he doth relate,
The chances of his past and present state;
Never was ear with Orpheus' harp possess'd
As her's with Jones, whilst he his life express'd.
Those that have warm'd themselves by these strong
   fires,
May eas'ly guess what fruits her wild desires
Produc'd to Jones; the observance of the court,
With feasts and banquets, and all princely sport,
Are at his foot: he cannot name nor wish
That meat he likes, but straight 'tis in his dish.
In this high state some months he takes his ease,
Whilst this sick Princess feeds on her disease:
At last a sharp alarm damps these desires,
Which threaten'd death, but could not quench her
   fires.
A Prince there was, mighty in bulk and mind,
Whose kingdom's confines unto No-land join'd:
Descended in his race from Og of Basan;
You'd think his very name might well amaze one,
Bahader Cham Mombaza's King; h' had been,
A long hot suitor to this mighty Queen,
But still repuls'd: now this unruly fire
Suppress'd with scorn, breaks forth from love to ire.
A mighty host he rais'd, and marcheth thro'
The heart of No-land, to command, not woo:
Approaching near her court, he sends her word,
She must be his own Queen at bed and board,
Or see her kingdom burn in higher flames
Than his for her: yet (for his spirit shames
To war with women) if she can find out
One man in all her realm, that is so stout,
In her defence with him his sword to try,
He'll bravely win her, or he'll bravely die.
Her courtiers quail'd at this, who knew his force,
Could not be parallel'd by man and horse.

Nor

Nor could it chufe but make the Queen look black,
Not pale. Th' interpreter at Jones his back,
Rounds in his ear this proud imperious fpeech;
Had fhe been thence, h' had bid him kifs his breech
For this proud meffage : up, howe'er, he ftarts,
And this loud anfwer with his mouth he farts ;
Go tell Bahader Cham Mombaza's King,
One Mars begot in's wrath will have a fling
With him ere night, that one who at one breath,
Don Dego and Gonzago did to death,
Will look him dead ; nor will I only be
This Princefs' champion, but (thy Cham to fee)
I'll walk thro' beds of fcorpions : for I hear
He dares enough, and I can broek no peer.
This high reply ne'er mov'd the haughty Cham,
Let Jones be what he will he's ftill the fame.
The day's his own before the fight's begun :
Were Mars himfelf inftead of Mars his fon.
A back and breaft and helmet ftrong he dond,
Well wrought and varnifh'd by fome Indian hand,
A whale-bone bow he takes of fpecial ftrength,
With arrows barb'd, at leaft two yards in length :
A crooked fcimiter whofe edge was flint,
Quaintly conjoin'd and fome tough fpell was in't,
To make it proof againft the ftrength of fteel.
Oft had this fword made head-ftrong Giants reel.
By his right fide a maffy mace he hangs,
With which his fturdy foes to death he bangs;
A buckler like a Spanifh ruff he wore
About his neck, full half yard deep, or more :
He wore not this for his defence, or grace,
But to keep off his urine from his face.
For you muft know that member was ftill mounted :
The braveft woman's man on earth accounted.
And thus prepar'd, this lufty termagant,
Afcends his caftle on his Elephant.
And then advanceth to a fpacious green,
Before the caftle of this maiden Queen.

I

A brave

A brave Arabian courfer is prepar'd
For Jones, his own true arms he dons for guard,
Llwellin's fword to do ; and fo defcends
Down to the Green, where the fierce Cham attends.
Jones was to feek what kind of fight were beft,
To make againft this Giant and his beaft.
Both far exceed in ftrength himfelf and horfe,
And therefore art muft now be join'd with force ;
Now breaft to breaft, a nimble charge, and gone,
His ready fteed as foon comes off as on.
Had not the well-try'd arms he wore prov'd true,
The Cham's fmart whale-bone bow had made him
  rue
This bold attempt: but what can whale's weak
  bones,
When whales themfelves came fhort to fwallow
  Jones ?
Thus thrice he charg'd, and thrice he came off clear,
At laft he came clofe up in full career,
And turning fhort, the horfe's hind feet flipp'd :
Thro' which mifchance the carry-caftle ripp'd
His bowels forth,with's tufk ; down falls the horfe :
The furious beaft clafp'd Jones with his probofce ;
And mounts him high ; but in his rife he found,
The means to give Bahader's face a wound,
And cuts in th'inftant off, the trunk that clafp'd him :
So down the Elephant was forc'd to caft him.
This hard exploit none ere perform'd before,
But one of Cæfar's * foldiers and no more.
The wounded beaft enrag'd with pain cries out
With hideous voice, and plung'd and pranc'd about
The Green, till from his feat the Prince he throw'th,
And then (for by the Cham from his firft growth,
This feat he had been taught) tho' mad with pain,
He ftrives to mount him on his back again.
But Jones had lopp'd off his ftrong trunk before,
Whereby he could perform this feat no more.

  * Read the Commentaries *De bello Africano.*

Here

Here Jones denies he bred this docile beaſt,
Taught to his hand, he got him to the Eaſt;
And his report muſt have belief before us,
Who ſwears it was the ſame that carry'd Porus *
Againſt the Macedon. I cannot ſee
How by wiſe Nature's rules this thing ſhould be,
Unleſs in Pliny's volumes it appears,
That Elephants may live two thouſand years.
Now Jones leaps up in haſte, and ſwiftly flies,
With ſword in hand, where bruis'd Bahader lies;
And ere he could get up, one waſhing ſtroke,
His head and buckler from his ſhoulders took;
Which when 'twas off, they may compare't that
   will,
To the grim St. John's head on Ludgate-Hill.
His numerous army ſtruck with grief and fright
At his ſad fate, betook itſelf to flight;
And thus was No-land's Queen redeem'd by Jones
From bondage, rape, and No-land's loſs at once.
Now if ſhe lov'd our Captain well before,
In reaſon ſhe muſt love him ten times more;
Which ſhe expreſs'd, by laying at his foot
Her people, No-land, and herſelf to boot:
But whether 'twas the god of love's deep curſe,
That ſhe refus'd for better, or for worſe,
Thoſe mighty Princes which to her he ſent,
To make her doat on a non-reſident;
Flings ſnow-balls at his heart, and flames at her's;
To keep conjunction from theſe errant ſtars;
Or whether Jones his genitals had got,
Some lame defect by Skink's late deſperate ſhot,
And ſo his noble heart made him refuſe,
What having got he could not rightly uſe.
'Tis not in me to judge, but this I know,
Her violent fires ſcorch'd her, and him his ſnow,

---

* Read Curtius touching that Elephant of Porus, who often remounted his maſter with his trunk in that battle between him and Alexander.

So cold that, to avoid her amorous fight,
He leaves her court, and fteals to fea by night :
So Jafon us'd Medea erft, but he's
So wife to take with him the golden fleece,
Which Jones contemn'd to do, and thought himfelf,
When fafe return'd, his country's mine of wealth.
No certain ground I have here to relate,
This great deferted Queen's unhappy fate ;
But Sir John Mandeville's, who doth deliver,
As Jones reports, he came foon after thither,
And found the people's outfide all in black ;
A fad expreffion for their Princefs' wreck.
Who told him lately there arriv'd a man,
All white, who for them wond'rous things had done.
Redeem'd their Queen and kingdom from the fhame
Of rape and rapine, which Bahader Cham
Came there to act, and was in open field,
By this white man in fingle combat kill'd.
Their Queen enamour'd with this matchlefs man,
Refus'd and left by him : when nothing can
Quench her wild fires but Carthage Queen's hard
    fate,
Whilft on the clift with penfive thoughts fhe fate,
A fudden fpring fhe gave, and fo commends
Herfelf to fea, where life and love fhe ends.
No more of this fad ftuff ; let's all at once
Join in a joyful welcome home to Jones.
In fix months fail he fteers by Goodwin fands,
Cafts anchor at the Downs ; the next day lands,
Haftes to the Queen at London, there expreffes
Every particular of his addreffes
To Prefter John; the great affairs fuccefs
As fhe defir'd : laftly, in his progrefs,
He might have married the great Queen of No-land,
But this the Queen gave credit to at no hand,
'Till 'twas confirm'd by Sir John Mandeville,
Whofe ftrange reports they may believe that will.
                                                    Now

Now let us well obſerve the happy fate,
Which ſtill provided for the Queen and ſtate.
Jones had not reſted fully three days here,
But out there breaks a great and fearful fire
Of ſtrong rebellion ; and to quench it, none's
So fit in common ſenſe, as Captain Jones.
Brave Eſſex thro' affronts turn'd malecontent,
Hatches in's breaſt a deſperate intent,
To ſeize the perſon of the Queen, and thoſe
He found moſt near about her his ſtrong foes.
Her Grace and counſel call for Jones, to know
What in his judgment now were beſt to do.
Who firſt her gracious pardon doth beſeech,
And then delivers this ſhort pithy ſpeech.
Firſt guard the Court with Weſtminſter's ſtrong
    bands,
Call in the neighbouring Counties by commands.
Out with your houſhold men, ſhut up your gates ;
We'll make your foes turn tail with broken pates.
Then call to you the richeſt of your Cits,
But ſeek no caſh ; for in their bags their wits
Are cloſe knit up ; but only thus much make
Them know, their wives and fortunes lye at ſtake ;
That they ſhall want no ſuccour, whilſt your hand
Can graſp the ſword, and ſceptre of this land.
Thus arm their hearts, and rouze them from their
    beds,
And then let us alone to arm their heads.
She now requires, that Jones in perſon go
To Eſſex, his intents to ſound and know ;
To uſe all faireſt means that may reduce him,
From thoſe lewd ways, to which loſt men ſeduce
    him.
He undertakes it ; haſtens to the Lord,
And is admitted in as ſoon as heard.
And here he finds Sir Walter Raleigh with him ;
Some ill was in't, his fancy ſtraight doth give him.
                                          He

He knew he came not to the Earl for good,
But to provoke him to some madder mood.
Therefore from thence our Jones doth Raleigh rate,
Shaking his martial truncheon o'er his pate:
Bids him pack thence to th' knaves of his Grand
    Jury,
He'll make him else th' example of his fury.
Raleigh was wise, and rul'd by his best sense;
Gives place to time, and so withdraws from thence.
Then Jones these counsels to the Earl began,
How full of dangers were the ways he ran.
How weak his power; much less unto the force
Of England's, than his rein-deer's to a horse.
Thus his brave family must be destroy'd,
His honour's lost, his ancient house made void:
Beside, his cause was naught; for tho' himself
Ne'er read the laws of this great Commonwealth,
Yet he had heard some Lawyer say long since,
There was no law to captivate our Prince.
Thus all the harmless blood that shall be spilt
In this bad cause, must lye on Essex guilt.
Lay hand on heart most noble Peer, (quoth Jones)
The Queen can pardon, and enrich at once.
Be you but good, she can be gracious,
Your own experience can inform you thus.
Thus Jones possess'd his noble heart so far,
He is resolv'd to wave the chance of war;
Himself and house he yields unto the Queen,
And her cold mercy, which too soon was seen.
This is the last great act I can relate,
Of his good service for the Queen and state:
Rewards fit for his worth there were prepar'd,
Which his high spirit pass'd by without regard:
And his great Queen was seriously bent,
To put him in some place of government;
But Nature only taught the man to fight,
And his rude mother not to read and write.

                                    Which

Which was the chiefeſt cauſe that made him hate,
To be employ'd in myſteries of ſtate.
Beſides, he was not pleas'd that her Grace,
Cut off this noble man before his face,
Whom he brought in ; it may be his own lot,
With axe or cord for nought to go to pot.
Thus ignorance, a diſcontented mind,
And worth ill weigh'd, do make him fall behind
Occaſion's lock ; which loſt, he never more,
Tho' bred and breath'd on hills, ſhall get before.
Now time and bruiſes, and much loſs of blood,
Had made Jones feel cold age was not ſo good
As fiery youth ; he needs muſt find a fail
Of what he was, declin'd from top to tail.
Which made him wiſh he might put up his reſt,
And breathe his laſt in his own country's breaſt.
And for this cauſe he went unto her Grace,
And begg'd of her a Muſter-maſter's place,
In Wales, near his firſt home ; where he may ſpend
His latter days in peace, and in it end :
And yet to leave behind his martial art,
To Wales' poſterity, before he part.
This ſuit with ſpeed and readineſs is granted,
And ſo to Wales our Muſter-maſter's jaunted.
Here many years he ſpent in telling more,
Or leſs of thoſe ſtrange things he did before :
At laſt in his old age he grows ſo wild,
He needs muſt marry, to beget a child.
Which tho' he miſs'd, the maſtery he muſt have
O'er every ſex, Jones ſent her to her grave.
Devotion now with his old age increaſt,
He meditates thrice every day at leaſt.
His only prayer was the Abſolution
In our old Liturgy, with ſome confuſion
Of ſhort ejaculations in his bed,
For ſome old ſlips, and for the blood he ſhed ;
Eſpecially for thoſe ſix Kings he kill'd,
Without remorſe at the Juzippian field :

At

At laſt death comes, whoſe power he defy'd,
From firſt to laſt, and thus he liv'd and dy'd.
　Now you wild blades that make looſe inns your
　　ſtage,
To vapour forth the acts of this ſad age,
Your Edghill fight, the Newberries and the Weſt,
And Northern claſhes, where you ſtill fought beſt :
Your ſtrange eſcapes, your dangers void of fear,
When bullets flew between the head and ear :
Your *pia maters* rent, periſh'd your guts,
Yet live, as then ye had been but earthen buts :
Whether you fought by damme, or the ſpirit,
To you I ſpeak, ſtill waving men of merit,
Be modeſt in your tales, if you exceed
My Captain's hard atchievements, I'll proceed
Once more to imp my rural Muſe's wings,
And turn my lyre ſo high, I'll break her ſtrings,
But I will reach ye, and thence raiſe ſuch laughter,
As ſhall continue for five ages after.

The CAPTAIN'S ELEGY.

AND art thou gone brave man ! hath conq'ring
　　death
Put a full period to thy bluſt'ring breath ?
Thus hath ſhe play'd her maſter-piece ? and here
Fix'd her *nil ſupra* on thy ſable bier ?
'Scap'ſt thou thoſe hideous ſtorms, thoſe horrid fights,
With many giants, cruel beaſts, fierce Knights ?
Such dangerous ſtratagems, ſuch foes intrapping,
And now hath death don't ? ſure ſhe took thee
　　napping ;
For had'ſt thou been awake to uſe thy ſword,
She would have ſhunn'd thee, and have ta'ne thy word
For thy appearance, till the laſt return
Of her long term.　Or did thy mettle burn,
Thro' thy chap'd clay unto Elyſium's ſhades,
T'' encounter with the ghoſts of thoſe old blades,
　　　　　　　　　　　　　　　　　　Great

Great Cæfar, Scipio, Hannibal; 'caufe here
Thy fiery fpirit could not find its peer?
How could'ft thou elfe find time to fold thy arms.
In thy ftill grave, now Mars rains bloody ftorms,
On Chriftian earth? great Auftria would be ours
Without pitch'd field, without beleaguring tow'rs:
Wert thou but here, thyfwordwould ftrike the ftroke,
To break or bring their neck to Britain's yoke.
Perhaps it was the providence of Fate,
To fnatch thee up, left thou fhoul'ft come too late,
Now foldiers drop, pell mell, whofe fouls might thruft
Thine from the chiefeft place, which thou from firft
Haft gain'd on earth; now what fhall England do?
Limp like fome grandame that hath loft her fhoe.
But cafe a new Tyrone again fhould fpring
From his old urn, no fome fuch furious thing
As fierce Mac-kill-cow, where were then our Jones,
To bring thefe rebels on their marrow-bones?
Or fay, 'gainft Spain our pikes we re-advance,
For their old fack, as fuch a thing may chance,
Where fhall we then find out that martial man,
That kill'd fix thoufand with nine fcore? he's gone.
And we that lick the difh that Homer lapt in,
What fury now fhall our dull brains be wrap'd in?
We muft go fing Sir Launcelot and rehearfe,
Old Huan's villainous profe in wilder verfe;
Or elfe put up our pipes, and all at once,
Cry farewel wit: all's gone with Captain Jones.
Well, go thy ways (old blade th' haft done thy fhare,
For things beyond belief time (never fear)
Will give thee being here: th' haft left us ftuff,
To build thy Pyramid, more than enough,
To equal Cair's, and happ'ly 'twill out laft it,
So with thy glorious deeds we may rough caft it;
Farewel great foul, and take this praife with many;
Except thy foes, thou ne'er did'ft harm to any:
And thus far let our Mufe thy lofs deplore,
Well fhe may figh, but fhe fhall ne'er fing more.

K   *His*

His E P I T A P H.

TREAD softly (mortals) o'er the bones,
Of the world's wonder Captain Jones:
Who told his glorious deeds to many,
But never was believ'd of any:
Posterity let this suffice,
He swore all's true, yet here he lyes.

F I N I S.

*B O O K S printed and sold by JOHN LEVER,
at Little Moorgate, next to London Wall, near
Moorfields.*

1. LOW LIFE, or one Half of the World knows not
how the other Half Live; being a critical Account of what is transacted by People of almost all Reli-
gions, Nations, Circumstances and Sizes of Understanding
in the Twenty-four Hours, between Saturday Night and
Monday Morning; in a true Description of a Sunday,
as it is usually spent within the Bills of Mortality, calcu-
lated for the 21st of June. With an Address to Mr. Hogarth. " Let Fancy guess the rest." Buckingham.
The Third Edition, adorned with a droll humorous
Print of St. Monday. Price only 1s. 6d.

2. THE SECRET HISTORY of Betty Ireland, who was
trepanned into Marriage at the Age of Fourteen, and
debauched by beau M——te, &c. &c. a Book full of
fur-

surprifing Incidents in the gay Life fhe paffed through, her Misfortunes, with her penitent and fudden Death. This Book is a proper Prefent to young People, to deter them from fuch Scenes of Life, that too many of the young and gay of both Sexes run into. The Seventh Edition, with a beautiful Frontifpiece of a Scene in gay Life. Price only 6d.

3. TABES DORSALIS, or the Caufe of Confumption in young Men and Women ; with an Explication of its Symptoms, Precautions, and the Method of Cure, &c. By a Phyfician of Briftol. The Fourth Edition, embellifhed with a curious Frontifpiece of a Gentleman and Lady in a deep Confumption. This Book is very proper for all Perfons to read in thefe fickly Times. *⁎* Be careful to afk for Lever's Book againft Confumptions. Price 1s.

4. THE ART OF SWIMMING. Illuftrated by Forty proper Copper Plate Cuts, which reprefent the different Poftures neceffary to be ufed in that Art, with Advice for Bathing. By Monfieur Thevenot, To which is prefixed, a prefatory Difcourfe concerning artificial Swimming, or keeping one's felf above Water, by feveral fmall portable Engines in cafe of Danger. The Second Edition. Price 1s. 6d. fewed, or 2s. bound. N. B. The Cramp is here provided againft, by a method in Swimming that will bring the Perfon in Safety to Shore ; for the Want of knowing which Secret, thoufands of Lives have been loft, as well as the experteft Swimmers, which will now be faved by reading this excellent Book.

5. THE HUSBAND forced to be Jealous ; or the Good Fortune of thofe Women that have jealous Hufbands ; being the fecret Hiftory of feveral noble Perfons. Tranflated from the French. The Second Edition, with a handfome Frontifpiece Cut of Gentlemen and Ladies. Price only 1s. N. B. This Book is on the Plan of Pamela, Clariffa, and Grandifon. *⁎* The many thoufands fold of the above Books in a few Month's Time, is a fufficient Teftimony of the Publick's Approbation.

6. THEOPHILUS CIBBER to David Garrick, Efq; with Differtations on Theatrical Subjects, Octavo, adorned with droll humorous Cuts. Price 4s. bound.

7. THE

7. THE PIOUS YOUTH's RECREATION, or Travels through Godlinefs; containing a pleafant Hiftorical Relation of the Families of Riches and Poverty, Godlinefs and Labour. Wherein the Family Neglects and Vices of Hufbands and Wives, Children and Parents, Mafters and Servants, are laid open in familiar Verfe, &c. Illuftrated with Diverfity of Pictures fuited to their feveral Occafions. Price only 6d. bound in gilt Covers.

8. SERMONS on Eleven important Subjects; to which is added a celebrated Latin Oration fpoken at Cambridge, by the pious Dr. Crowe, of Bifhopfgate Church, London, and late Chaplain to the King. Octavo, 4s. bound.

9. LATIN GRAMMAR, by JOHN READ, of Bofton in New England. Price 3d. ftitched.

10. THE BLOODY TRIBUNAL, or an Antidote againft Popery; being a Review of the horrid Cruelties of the Inquifition, as practifed in Spain, Portugal, Italy, and the Eaft and Weft Indies, on all thofe whom the Church of Rome brands with the Name of Hereticks. Extracted from Authors of undoubted Credit, and embellifhed with Copper Plate Cuts, Octavo, bound.

11. A PLAIN ADDRESS to the Followers and Favourers of the Methodifts, by the late Reverend Mr. Anguifh, of Deptford in Kent. Price 4d.

12. BRUIN IN THE SUDS; or Mafonry Vindicated. Being a Poetical Narrative of a late famous Trial of Skill between a noted Vintner and a Lodge of Free Mafons, cooked up in a Song. Price 6d.

13. A DISSERTATION on Mr. HOGARTH's Six Prints, viz. Gin Lane, Beer Street; and the Four Stages of Cruelty. Being a proper Key for the right Apprehenfion of the Author's Meaning in thofe celebrated Defigns, with a Print of Mr. Hogarth in a Drawing Attitude. Price 1s.

14. AN HISTORICAL DEDUCTION of Government, in a Letter to a Friend in the Country. By Sir Tanfield Leman, Bart. Price 6d.

15. THE TRIAL OF CAPTAIN G——, for Crim. Con. with Ad——l K——s's Lady, which was tried in the Court of King's Bench at Guild-hall, by a Special Jury, on Saturday the 11th of June 1757, when one thoufand Pounds Damages were given to the Plaintiff, with the original Letters. The Sixth Edition, 1s.